This collective is dedicated to all the women who (
Dreams are meant to be lived. Don't be too shy
touch the stars! Find a mentor and then bec

Many years ago, a young lady approached me about buying an ad in a magazine and we became fast friends! She sold me ads for years and her daughter attended LearningRx with amazing changes.

One day, in discussion, her dream of owning her own magazine was discovered and discussed and challenged. She took the step out and with lots of love and encouragement from those of us who knew her potential, her dream became a reality.

Bevin, I am so proud of the wonderful work you undertook and I cannot say enough about it. You are more like a daughter to me than a friend. You are a dreamer and an action taker. You are learning and growing into a magnificent business woman and look how far you have come! LolaMagazine has embraced the best of the women in Louisiana. You are thriving while making a difference as well as an example for your daughter.

The stars are yours!

The Collective:
Articles Written by Donesa Walker

Written by: Donesa Walker
Design by: Will Baten

Table of Contents

READY, SET, LEARN

Tips to Engage the Brain in the Learning Process

By Donesa Walker, M.Ed
Owner of LearningRx
of Shreveport-Bossier

Queuing up in a line for a concert or a much anticipated movie premier holds no candle to getting all ready for the first day back to school whether you are a child or an adult. This preparation takes place on many levels such as school supplies, clothing, books, travel arrangements, changing waking/sleeping schedules, etc. However, there is one area that is often overlooked and this is the cueing up of the learning process itself. While many students gear up excitedly, other students experience a high level of anxiety at the onset of the school year and some even get very sick at the prospect of another school day. The brain, unlike other organs/muscles in the body, experiences emotion and associates events/places with these emotions. Helping all students to anticipate school as a positive thing is a big challenge and each parent/guardian has his/her hands full. Being ready is the key. Let's look at this as if preparing for a vacation; after all, that's a fun thing to look forward to with anticipation and not fright.

READY

Preparing for a trip requires planning and foresight. Apply the same to preparing for the school year. Most prepare for the school year by simply getting school supplies, clothing, etc. and don't make this necessary first step. Starting the year off by getting checkups is important. Schedule checkups promptly with medical doctors for vision, hearing, dental, and others as needed. If the student has never struggled with the learning process but is involved in sports, this is also a good time to get a baseline cognitive assessment for awareness of the brain function and the learning process. If the student has struggled in the past with learning experiences, this is the right time to get a cognitive & academic assessment to screen for any learning difficulties so that you can add any interventions needed in the school setting to your success plan for the new school year as well as schedule outside interventions as necessary. A cognitive assessment is simply a series of tests that assess the way a student of any age learns best and allows the parent/guardian/student to know the learning style, strengths and weaknesses. Achieving awareness of these skills is much like getting a health checkup for vision, hearing, etc. Being armed with this knowledge allows good planning for a successful year. Cognitive assessments are available formally through local psychologists & counselors when seeking a diagnosis and are often covered by insurance. These assessments are available informally as well as locally. Additionally, some online versions are also available such as The Gibson Test of Cognitive Skills. In some instances, when intervention is needed or just desired for a leg up, getting brain training to retrain the thinking skills to a higher efficiency and enhance the learning process is the right step. There are local tutoring agencies to boost academic content areas also which sometimes getting a head start in these areas can benefit the student. Every student should know the direction of their learning processes so mapping the school year ahead will not be as frightful.

SET

Sit down with the student(s) and tentatively plan out the school year. Remember if you have multiple students in the household, a "family" meeting about this may be necessary to coordinate travel and extra-curricular especially if an older student is responsible for a younger sibling. Print out a school calendar with starting dates, vacation dates, etc. for each student so each student has his/her own plan. Discuss expectations for the year such as grades, homework, performance in sports and extra-curricular. Let the student(s) lead the plan with the parent/guardian contributing and guiding these conversations. Discuss reward "souvenirs" for meeting expectation goals. Discuss consequences in advance for not meeting expectations as this will lead to a smoother disciplinary intervention. Be deliberate. Discuss concerns and anxiety inducers, and then try to alleviate these in simple manners. For some students, driving to the new campus and walking around it will reduce anxiety. Most schools will allow students to "tour" their campus if you call ahead and make arrangements. Make sure to include nutritional awareness to the plan. It is so important to the brain that the student stays ade-

quately hydrated which means drinking water often throughout the school day. Make a plan with the student to track this intake as hydrating the body is the number one way to combat short term memory loss especially in the hot days of the summer season when school starts. Students who participate in sports really need to be aware of the level of water intake in the body as dehydration leads to a lot of health issues long term. Organize student study area, homework area, backpack and school planner/binder. Make a plan for when these items will be "checked" by the parent/guardian and set expectations for this in advance.

LEARN

A week to two weeks before school, begin the early sleep schedule, nutritional schedule, media schedule and study practices that student will use during the school year so that the student(s) form these healthy habits. Build excitement into the day by preparing special notes and snacks that will refresh the student throughout the day. If student is on medication that is used only during the school year, begin implementing it into the routine as often student may have a need for a medication change or update as growth occurred over the summer holidays. Make it a habit for parent/guardian to write a note of encouragement to the student to go into backpack or lunchbox each day. Preparing these in advance can help assure that each day one is included. Follow up each day. Have student/parent conversation that includes deliberate

probing questions. Avoid the following questions: How was your day? What did you do today? Be specific in your questions. Ask questions such as the following: What new things did you learn in Math today? Who made you feel happy today? When did you enjoy your day the most? Ask specific subject- related questions on test days rather than generic "How did the test go?" The number one indicator to student success is parental involvement. Read to the student every day! No matter what age the student is, reading aloud builds a sense of togetherness like nothing else as well as refining vocabulary and allows the parent/guardian opportunities to speak into the student's life about values, morals, etc. Sharing a great book builds a relationship that can last a lifetime.

WIN!!

Remember every student is a winner every day even on those days where the parent/guardian feels frustrated. Student behavior both academic and emotional relies on a training mindset. "Train up a child in the way he should go and when he is older, he will not depart from it." Proverbs 22:6. Training students to think with heart, soul and mind is the ultimate challenge and the proof is evident as the student grows and learns. Pouring into the student morals, beliefs, and learning requires time.

*Remember
to a child Love
is spelled
TIME!*

AN ALTERED STATE OF MIND

Donesa Walker, M.Ed, is the owner of LearningRx of Shreveport-Bossier.

Overcoming Struggles with Learning Disorders

"Issues with School failure, low self-esteem, early drug use and higher rates of juvenile delinquency" quotes The Advocate of Dr. Steven Felix, a Louisiana pediatrician are all side effects of learning disorders especially that of ADHD, and yet Louisiana has over 18% of our kids diagnosed with ADD/ADHD and the highest percentage in the nation of kids on meds for this disorder according to a recent study. Over 10% of our state's kids are on ADD meds and this is simply unacceptable with the long term side effects and results. Additionally, Dyslexia and other related disorders now affect as much as 15-20% of our kids in Louisiana. That's 1 in 5 kids or 4-5 kids per classroom. 2 out of 5 kids are not reading at grade level by 4th grade according to the Nation's report card and this rate is even higher in LA. The effects of ADD/ADHD, dyslexia, dysgraphia, dyscalculia, etc. on our economy are overwhelming. Dr. Sandra Chapman of The Center for Brain Health at the University of Texas in Dallas calls it BRAINOMICS and cites that the cost of cognitive deficits leading to learning disorders is an economic crisis we must address. Enough with the bad news! Let's get busy correcting this trend.

How to make change? First, understand that ADHD is a brain disorder which has symptoms including difficulty completing tasks, impulsiveness, being restless and compulsive, all of which many struggle with at various points in their lives. Dyslexia along with its partners, dyscalculia and dysgraphia are also brain disorders with a wide range of symptoms that are growing in our population. Additionally, environmental factors including television, smart phones and computer usage as well as more severe factors such as poverty induced nutritional deficits, neglect/abuse, and exposure to alcohol/drugs in the womb and in early life all lead to a higher rate of occurrence. Louisiana ranks at the very bottom in several areas on the Nation's Report Card as of current research released in August 2016. It is hard to educate a population struggling with so many factors contributing to learning delays, but it can be done.

Second, we must take community ownership by stepping up to partner with community efforts such as STEP FORWARD that are striving to make inroads in these areas of concern and give of our time to be a community partner.

Third, we must take steps in our own lives to diligently address the environmental factors we have within our control such as dietary options-eating more leafy greens and nuts to increase our magnesium intake. Did you know that a magnesium deficit has the same symptoms of ADD?

Are you getting an adequate amount into your diet or taking a supplement to enhance your brain performance? 80% of Americans are not getting enough into their diet through regular means. In society today, there are alternate ways to get this into your system such as lotions, oils, and over the counter minerals but nothing beats eating it naturally. Another environmental factor we must address is overuse of technology in our lives. Have you honestly charted how much time you & your children spend on smartphones, televisions, computers, etc? Is the WIFI constantly running in your home? The American Academy of Pediatrics has recommended that a child use only 10 minutes of data streaming (technology) times the age of the child and none at least one hour prior to bed. So for the under 1 year age, that's no TV! For the elementary aged child, that means only 1 hour or less of technology including video games daily and definitely not any 1 hour before bed. In this techno-age, many children spend hours each day gleaning information from technology and even in some cases have textbooks gone to tablets. So how do you combat this techno-age and keep our brains healthy? Train the brain. You are training your brain every moment of every day in some way but a deliberate approach is recommended to reverse the effects of too much/too little of all.

What are some ways to train the brain effectively and efficiently? One way is simply a family game night. This is a simple solution that addresses ways the brain learns. Another way is to partner with a brain trainer via a local training facility such as LearningRx so you can be guided in the correct games/activities for your child's brain. Getting a cognitive assessment so you know how your child's brain learns is the key. Third, you can read every night to your child no matter what their age as this builds vocabulary and social interaction skills. Fourth, you can use the 1 hour of techno time for valuable brain training games aimed at your child's ability by choosing wisely at Learningworksforkids.com or stop by LearningRx to pick up a FREE game pack and/or list of 100 APPS that are good for the brain (these are also available for download online on the website www.learningrx.com/shreveport).

Finally, combating a learning disorder whether you are an adult or a child starts with positive steps to address it and being deliberate about taking charge of your own abilities. Don't let weaknesses overwhelm you. Address them. Don't let excuses rule your life. Instead make a deliberate plan to boost your brain and that of your children, parents, etc. The growth long term is worth the time and effort now.

For more information: contact Donesa Walker at LearningRx Shreveport-Bossier. 318.797.8523 or email us to receive the free game packs at Shreveport.la@learningrx.net. *Lola*

QUICK TIPS *for* ADHD & DYSLEXIA

Identify the Cognitive weaknesses by getting an assessment-available via local psychologists and through LearningRx. LearningRx does NOT diagnose learning disorders but only looks at the weak cognitive skills to individualize a brain training intervention.

- Limit technology reasonably - 10 min x age of child or not more than 3 hours daily for adults.

- Boost nutritional benefits of magnesium & other minerals via a healthy diet-ask your doctor or see a lifestyle physician.

- Drink plenty of water to combat short term memory loss-example: 100lbs=50oz water daily.

- Read with your child/family members daily/nightly & play rhyming games, word games, and vocabulary building games often.

- Family game night playing board games that boost brain skills-list available from LearningRx.

- Engage in purposeful brain training-either with a personal trainer (LearningRx) or via a deliberate approach.

- For ADD/ADHD, try alternate treatment methods such as behavioral therapy versus medication or with medication as recommended by your doctor.

- For dyslexia, get engaged with intervention programs such as LearningRx , Masonic Lodge programs, A Kids Choice Foundation or working with a speech/language specialist as well as those offered by your local school.

- Keep a positive mindset and Switch on Your Brain per Dr. Caroline Leaf by engaging in positive thought and restatements during the harder times.

Smarter Games & Toys
for Smarter Girls & Boys

WRITTEN BY DONESA WALKER, M.ED,
OWNER OF LEARNINGRX OF SHREVEPORT-BOSSIER

Cognitive skills can change!

Kids can get smarter and so can adults through simple interventions such as brain training and simply by playing games that challenge their thinking processes both online and family game style! The key to everything is intensity and moderation.

Think of exercise for the body. A benefit can be had from a friendly game of volleyball or soccer in the front yard or a daily swim in the pool however, a greater benefit is had if it is intentional and regular. This doesn't mean that you have to play the same games over and over-quite the opposite! To challenge the brain, up the ante each time the game is played by using a timer or counting or change to different games with the same skill set in mind. For example, a great game of tic-tac-toe can be played by most anyone, and it can be challenging by just a little tweak such as having to count to five while making the play on your turn and having to do it within that count of five or by a simple change of playing it with numbers or letters instead of Xs and Os.

Let's explore the benefits and tweaks to make the games a little more exciting and challenging for true brain growth in a few of the "regular" games we have around the house on the holidays. Uno is a great game of numbers and can be made much more beneficial to the brain by simply adding a counting or speed to it. This game works the short term memory, processing speed and number/letter recognition while having fun as well as a myriad of other skills such as attention and focus. By simply adding a timing factor to it, the intensity is raised to challenge even the best player. If an adult who is quite skilled is playing with a child, the adult could have to make a decision by counting aloud to 3 and playing while the child gets to count to 10 while playing. -This playing. This evens the playing field and makes it a mental challenge for both players as well as a fun laugh when someone loses a turn for not playing quick enough!

Another fun game of strategy is checkers. I love getting those big mats with the enormous checkers out to play with all the nieces and nephews! Challenge the game up a level by using the same timing activity mentioned above or making a rhyme ongoing. First player must say a food, then the next player on his/her turn must list another food of the same food group, color, or rhyme a word with it.

Most everyone can remember the old Rhythm game-snap, snap, clap, clap, rhythm; name some kinds of ice cream…. Well, this game is a classic oldie but a goodie! This game has turned into a new game of categorizing like Scattergories and five second rule. These games are great for boosting that long term memory recall. One can always play the easy homemade game of alphabet in the car on long trips or at a family game time. Name animals that start with letters of the alphabet-A: Anteater, B: Bear, etc. recalling what all the previous persons listed on every fifth letter adds to the challenge.

The main point is that game time with the family creates memories, relationship, fun conversation, social engagement and grows the brain at the same time. Games are always great gifts to purchase and last long beyond the moment! Classic games can be bought, made, enhanced or embellished very simply. Get your game on and plan a fun family holiday time!

LearningRx is happy to give you a list of games on the next page, as well as to make a downloadable game gift pack available to any who come by or ask. LearningRx is also having a Smart Toy Box giveaway in December. Sign up and one lucky family will enjoy game time with a winning box full of games. Additionally, a great gift to give is the Gift of LearningRx brain training/ assessments (Assessments are discounted this month to $195-regular price is $299 and Brain Training Special Trial packages are only $299 for 6 hours). With any assessment booked in November and December, the parent/client will receive a wrapped game for giving. *Lola*

Best Games by Category

BOARD GAMES:

5 second Rule, Checkers/Chess, SET, Scattergories Card Game, Scrabble Slam Card Game, Uno, Punderdome, Blokus, Taboo, Spot It, Farkle, Catchphrase, Scrimish, KerPlunk, Connect 4, ThinkFun Rush Hour, Phase10, Rummikub, Sequence, Masterpiece Tetris, etc. For a complete list, see a specialist at LearningExpress Toys, or Come by LearningRx to get a GamePack list.

VIDEO GAMES:

Mindcraft, Tetris, Brain Games, games that involve strategy such as Starcraft or others that mimic real world decision making can be beneficial on a moderate level such as Flight Simulator , Farm Simulator and Sim City. See www.raisesmartkid.com for a complete list.

SMART APPS:

Rhyme Zone, Chain of Thought, Bejeweled, Proverbidioms. Try www.LearningWorks for Kids.com which can individualize the best apps for your child.

CAR GAMES:

Alphabet Game, card games like Uno, Spot It, Catchphrase electronic, IQFit, Total Brian Workout book, Simon electronic. A complete list as well as a Game Pack is available for free download at www.learningrx.com/shreveport.

HOMEMADE GAMES:

Memory, the pattern game, opposite day, tell a creative story in just 7 words, I spy, counting backwards, spelling words backwards, recreating a room visually… for a complete list, see Pinterest Post by LearningRx.

"I Just Can't Take It Anymore!"

Calming the Anxious Brain to Increase Performance

WRITTEN BY DONESA WALKER, M.ED, OWNER OF LEARNINGRX OF SHREVEPORT-BOSSIER

Anxiety can be a debilitating condition. Anxiety changes chemicals in your brain that can affect the way you think and the way you feel to such a degree that each thought feels normal or can become overwhelming. People struggle to tell themselves that they're worrying for no reason, but anxiety tells them that their worry makes sense. Anxiety makes them genuinely feel there are issues to worry about. It does this by negative thinking. It's the act of genuinely believing that something negative is going to occur because of the way anxiety affects your brain. Most detrimental stress comes from the overanxious brain and can lead to physical inhibitions and depression. This is especially true for a pattern of anxious behavior that can lead to anxiety attacks that can physically shut down the body and make a person ill. The chemical changes in the brain can be responsible for an overall shut down effect on the body, but you can control your anxiety by dealing with the stress in advance as it begins to occur. Academic and social performance both in school and on the job are greatly impacted by anxiety.

HERE ARE SIX TIPS TO DEALING WITH ANXIETY AND TO STAVE OFF ANXIETY ATTACKS BEFORE THE CHEMICAL CHANGE OCCURS IN THE BRAIN.

■ **PRAYER/MINDFULNESS** – Centering your thoughts outside yourself and on nature, God, the beauty around you and focusing on these have a cleansing effect on the brain and allow the brain's neurons to problem solve in a relaxed manner. Over time, people who engage in this centering process of prayer and meditation develop thicker layers of neurons in the attention-focused parts of the prefrontal cortex and in the insula, an area that's triggered when we tune into our feelings and bodies. Other research has shown that being mindful boosts activation of the left prefrontal cortex, which suppresses negative emotions, and minimizes the activation of the amygdala which is the "alarm" trigger for fight or flight. To reduce fight/flight once it has started, begin to think small to large-my fingers are fine, my toes are ok, my arms are ok, etc. until you reach your core....As in Philippians 4:8, Think on these things: things that are true, honest, just, pure, good reports...."

■ **POSITIVE JOURNALING** – Preventative measure-write down good uplifting thoughts such as scriptures that can combat anxiety and put into places that you will see them when you are facing the anxiety such as on your bathroom mirror, refrigerator, dashboard of your car, on your child's notebook, in your child's lunch sack, etc. "I can do all things through Christ who strengthens me".

■ SURROUND YOURSELF WITH POSITIVE PEOPLE –

"Birds of a feather flock together." Positive thinking friends have a profound influence on your mental health and the negative ninnies do too. Locate people that act the way you want to feel and spend time with them. If you find positive relationships, you'll become more positive around them and it spreads. Smiles are contagious. If you have a solitary job or situation, find positive videos/pictures that make you smile and laugh. Laughter is good medicine for the soul.

■ SOCIAL MEDIA DIET –

Take time off from negative feeds in your social media account-stay away from negative people and negative press by suppressing your feed to those that are not uplifting in what they post, or stay off the social web altogether to re-center yourself.

■ ATTAINABLE GOAL SETTING –

A sense of accomplishment is also a great tool for positivity. Set many different small attainable goals for yourself. Reaching these goals shows you that you worked for something, which is a great way to overcome anxiety. One such goal can be to overcome negative thought by practicing positive restatement because if you're able to overcome anxiety you'll be able to overcome negative thinking. But in the meantime, focusing on becoming a more positive person can have profound results for your day to day happiness.

■ EXERCISE COGNITIVELY AND PHYSICALLY–

Both mental and physical exercise create positivity. When your brain/body feel healthy, your mind releases more "good mood" neurotransmitters that help you deal with some of the symptoms of anxiety. Setting up a quick walk or a mental exercise to do when anxiety strikes allows you to think ahead and combat negative feelings before they can take root. Perhaps counting backwards from 100 by 2s…spelling your city backwards…even singing songs that are old tunes that you have to recall the words also opens up the neurons to fire in a positive manner-Think of Little Orphan Annie singing Tomorrow…the sun will come out tomorrow…or the cute little mice singing "somewhere over the rainbow"… or grandma singing "Jesus never Fails "Exercising the brain in a positive manner gets those neurons firing and bundling together which causes endorphins to boost, and you can have a little chocolate (serotonin) to boot without guilt if you have exercised that body!

Stress doesn't have to be a bad thing and can actually be quite good for the body as it makes us work more quickly and diligently. When the pressure becomes a level of stress/anxiety that our body and mind cannot handle, then the chemical changes occur and become detrimental to our health and well-being. Scripture tells us that God has not given us a Spirit of Fear but of Love and a sound mind so we need to practice this in our everyday life. There are all kinds of simple tools from scents/oils such as peppermint to soothe to professionals that have psychology and counseling degrees as well as medications to help. If you are struggling with extremes, seek out a professional and be upfront with what you are feeling. If you need a brain trainer to boost your academic and cognitive thought processes, seek out LearningRx or other local professionals. If you need spiritual help, find a good local church with an active positive group of people to interact with and engage yourself and your family. Boost your performance by taking steps in advance to reduce anxiety load and see if you don't feel better in 2017! *Lola*

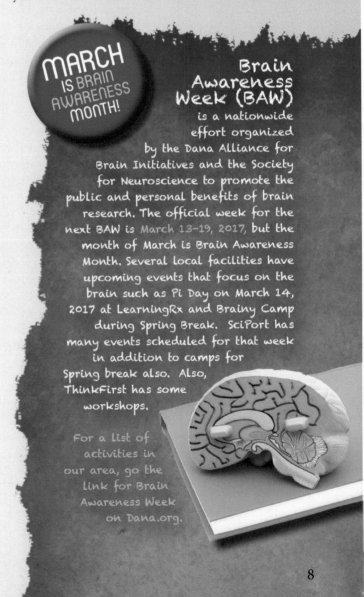

MARCH IS BRAIN AWARENESS MONTH!

Brain Awareness Week (BAW) is a nationwide effort organized by the Dana Alliance for Brain Initiatives and the Society for Neuroscience to promote the public and personal benefits of brain research. The official week for the next BAW is March 13-19, 2017, but the month of March is Brain Awareness Month. Several local facilities have upcoming events that focus on the brain such as Pi Day on March 14, 2017 at LearningRx and Brainy Camp during Spring Break. SciPort has many events scheduled for that week in addition to camps for Spring break also. Also, ThinkFirst has some workshops.

For a list of activities in our area, go the link for Brain Awareness Week on Dana.org.

Beatin' the Heat & Skippin' out on the SUMMER Brain Drain

WRITTEN BY DONESA WALKER, M.ED, OWNER OF LEARNINGRX OF SHREVEPORT-BOSSIER

Having a fun summer time and still staying sharp for another school year is an important task that seems to bombard every parent each year. Picking the right summer camps and activities that stimulate the brain and are still fun puts a lot of pressure on parents and grandparents. But Summer Fun doesn't have to include a Summer Slide of learning skills. For a few simple ways to celebrate the summer, simply think back to the long summers of your childhood. There are simple things within your grasp in your community that stimulate brain activity and even a thing or two in this new-fangled technological world that can plug that drain too. Take a few notes, cut out an idea or two and simply have fun!

First, don't be afraid of your child being BORED! Boredom actually creates innovation. I remember some of the best memories of my life came from the days I was so bored that I had to get creative. Pull out a memory or two from your childhood of lazy summer days reading a book, playing jacks on the front porch, chasing fireflies in the dark, telling creative ghost stories around a camp fire…share these with your child/grandchild. Storytelling is a lost art that never gets old. Break out your talent and be wild with your memories for these are priceless. The best thing about summer to me is reading and what child/teen/adult could not benefit from that adventure.

HERE ARE A FEW SITES OFFERING RECOMMENDATIONS ON GOOD MATERIALS to make the mind soar:

- http://www.guysread.com/ (for boys by guys)
- http://www.amightygirl.com/books for girls (lots of other stuff for girls there too)
- https://www.goodreads.com/list/tag/teen (teens-choose wisely)
- https://www.scholastic.com/teachers/blog-posts/genia-connell/100-books-build-character/ (books to build character in your child)

Another idea is to Create a "Bored" box. Put in the box things that remind you of your childhood-even the box itself and when your child says, "I'm Bored", give them the box, have them pull an item out, and then let them creatively use that item. Or if you don't have a lot of childhood memories of fun times, put small things in that can creatively get the juices flowing-a coloring book & crayons, a stuffed animal and a blanket, a bag of marshmallows and a large bar of chocolate (or just a picture of a recipe for the smaller kids). Put small blocks and tiny figurines in with some toys and some "Easter" grass so they can form a fairy garden or a war zone. Fill a show box up with some "dollar toys" or some of their own toys they haven't played with in a while, and wrap it or have them play guess what it is. Put in some of your old clothes for "dress-up", some old socks to use for sock puppets, etc. Let your imagination go wild for a minute and then when they are bored, you can show them how fun imagination really is! Here's a great website to try: http://mothers-home.com/85-activity-ideas-for-bored-kids/

If you are having trouble with this idea, then try a deck of cards or two. There are some really great card games that can be played with a deck of cards that most people have in their house. Everything from sorting by color to putting in order by number to poker! https://www.pagat.com/ this website offers hundreds of card game ideas with a simple deck of cards. However, there are also many other types of card games that rock too! Uno, Scrabble Slam, Scattergories, Rook, Phase10, & WhizKids are some of my favorites. I can remember all the evenings growing up when my parents invited other families over to our house and they all sat down to play Mille Bornes-a fun, fast-paced game about driving a car to a destination at the fastest speed you could manage all in a deck of cards!!! It is still my most favorite of all time. (yes, I know -I did it on purpose for the grammar police out there).

Another great inspiring and potentially family building experience is game night. Family game night can do wonders for the brains of your kids and for you! Other board games that challenge the mind can take longer and work on strategy which ultimately enhances the logic & reasoning skills needed in upper math skills. Some of these include Connect4, Checkers, Chess and the ultimate RISK! Monopoly and Life still stand out as the games of the decade in my teens (oops! Revealing my age there). Some other board games that are great for the brain are found here- http://www.lifehack.org/articles/lifestyle/15-fun-board-games-that-exercise-your-brain-and-make-you-smarter.html. Or http://learningrxreviews.com/category/games/ (5 second Rule rocks in the home or on the road-I even use it at work!)

So, vacation time has arrived and as you hit the road, you make sure the DVD player is loaded with all the DVDs the car can hold as well as all the video game paraphernalia to keep the, "Are we there yet?" manageable, but here are a few Car Games to try instead that build that wonderful imagination in your child's brain and challenge that memory to grow. Build a Story in the Car: This game starts with the phrase, "In the car there was….." The first person fills in the blank with anything, such as, "A French goat." The next person repeats that and adds another object or phrase; "In the car there was a French goat cooking on a George Forman Grill." The game ends when one of the players forgets part of the story. Encourage kids to picture the scene and try to connect the vivid images. The sillier the images, the better! This helps them to build the mental skills of long-term memory and divided attention. Another way to play is the first person starts the list with a word (rather than a phrase) that starts with "A", the next person repeats the "A" word and adds a "B" word, then a "C" word, etc. Another game is I Spy a Sound: the first person begins with the phrase, "I spy something that starts with the 'S' sound. The other players take turns guessing, and between each guess they get another sound clue, such as, "I see something that starts with the 's' sound and is the color that starts with the 'r' sound." This revved-up version of the old favorite helps with logic and reasoning and promotes auditory process skills. Again, a good variation is to progress in alphabetical order as above, with subsequent hints given without regard to beginning sounds (although extra points might be awarded for doing so!). And there's always the license plate game and many others. http://www.minitime.com/trip-tips/10-Best-Car-Games-for-Kids-article

When all else fails and you child just has to have some Tech Time-go for the apps that are good for the brain. LearningRx offers a list of 100 apps that are good for the brain, and you can call us or email us to get that for free. Shreveport.la@learningrx.net or you can see a few here http://learningrxreviews.com/category/apps/ but my favorite is a personalized list from http://learningworksforkids.com/. Here you can enter your child's things he or she needs to work on and they give you a personalized list of apps/games to build those skills. So cool!

Finally, the camps!!! There are so many amazing camps that feature some really great options in our community. There are day camps and VBS opportunities galore. Check out the lists that are here in Lola for just a few of the stellar ones in our area-(my favorite are the brainy ones, but I might be partial). Most of all, enjoy every moment because these days are fleeting and even listening to," I'm Bored," is missed when they head off to college and beyond..... *Lola*

COGNITION IGNITION
WHAT IS COGNITION & HOW DOES IT AFFECT LEARNING PROCESSES AT ALL AGES?

WHAT IS COGNITION?

Cognition is the umbrella term for your learning skills—your ability to process information, reason, remember, and relate. In short, your cognitive skills are your thinking skills. When you struggle to process or think through information, this causes a weakness in your thinking efficiency and this is known as a cognitive deficiency. Cognitive skills impact the way we learn, the efficiency of the learning process and what we do with the information that we have learned.

WHAT IMPACTS COGNITION?

Many factors play into your growth of cognitive skills such as genetics, proper hydration & nutrition, overall health, and aging are among those that have the highest affect as well as activities that impact the brain such as playing sports or getting concussions. Strengthening or weakening of cognitive skills happens sometimes by choices we make in lifestyle as well as things that are outside our control but there has never been a better time to be aware of our own cognitive function that in the high stress, fast paced world full of technological advances & pitfalls.

HOW DOES THIS AFFECT OUR LEARNING PROCESSES?

Examining some of the ways we can make better choices to take charge of our own brain health starts when we are young and continues through all ages. Being aware of our own brain fitness is imperative to having the best in our society. Statistics state that those with higher cognitive function actually have higher income over their lifetime and this makes brain health a high priority. Dr. Sandra Chapman with University of Texas at Dallas Center for Brain Health coined the term "Brainomics" to define the high economic cost of poor brain performance, and she sees brain health and enhancement as the most significant path through which to raise the standard of living globally. As quoted in the Reader's Digest in August 2017 & on the UT brain health website, "Although the origins of intelligence are still being researched, it does seem clear that IQ, or intelligence quotient, is not fixed—it can change throughout your life. Studies show our nutrition and other environmental factors may also impact brain power. We used to think that once smart, always smart and vice versa—we now know that is wrong," says Sandra Bond Chapman, PhD, founder and chief director of the Center for Brain Health at The University of Texas at Dallas. "Science clearly reveals that the brain and our 'smartness' are anything but fixed. We continuously shape and rewire our brain by how we think."

If we can change how we think and our choices impact how we learn, what can we do to make our learning processes easier especially if we already have learning or memory deficits? Just like exercise is necessary for the body, so it necessary for the brain. The more deliberate we are about addressing the specific areas of weakness the better improvements we will experience. The first step is to truly identify which skills are weak. Getting a cognitive checkup such as that given by LearningRx & other local providers is very important to understanding your cognitive health.

Recently, I went to the dentist for a complete checkup and I found out that I had more than one cavity trying to develop not because I was doing anything bad for my teeth but more because I wasn't doing what I needed to in order to give them all the care they needed to stay healthy. I knew immediately what things I needed to do as well to take care of my dental health.

WHEN IS THE LAST TIME YOU HAVE HAD A CHECKUP FOR YOUR COGNITIVE FUNCTION?

In a recent meeting of the World Economic Forum, of 3000+ decision makers, 84% of them agree that adults of all ages should take charge of their own brain function without waiting for a doctor to tell them to do so as well as 83% saying they should getting an annual mental checkup and 94% say brain health should be a healthcare priority.

WHAT'S THE NEXT STEP?

Once you have identified your cognitive strengths and weaknesses, then you must take charge of enhancing those skills that are weak through targeted exercises either digitally, with a personal brain trainer, or through concerted discipline via games & activities at home depending on the gain level you desire or need. Do your research and take charge of your mental health! Cognition is the engine to your learning! Time to rewire and rev up no matter what your age!!

WRITTEN BY DONESA WALKER, M.ED, OWNER OF LEARNINGRX OF SHREVEPORT-BOSSIER

A Race Against Time:

BOOSTING PROCESSING SPEED IN THE BRAIN

WRITTEN BY DONESA WALKER, M.ED, OWNER OF LEARNINGRX OF SHREVEPORT-BOSSIER

Ever had one of those days where it seemed everything was running in slow motion, you felt constantly behind schedule, and your brain just couldn't keep up with the demand? I've heard the dog days of summer are like that and leave us with a feeling of malaise, but a lot of times it is really a matter of slower brain function known as processing speed. Everyone wants that fastest phone, computer, upload speed, but not many people are willing to put in the time and effort it takes to boost the old cognition. Processing speed is defined as the speed at which the brain maximizes the learning processes for both new and old information flow. How quick are you at remembering details such as your grandmother's maiden name? The brain has to do several processes to get that information out of "Ye old filing cabinet" of long term memory and access that data for a full load. Are you having trouble remembering passwords quickly or accessing names to link to faces of people you know at a rapid speed? These are all signs of aging and the processing speed slowing down. As the brain ages, the load of information it carries becomes burdensome, and it takes a little longer to think through processes than it did when we were young whippersnappers! So what can be done?

Boosting processing speed is much like preparing for a marathon. You know how to run or ride that bike, but you must train and gradually increase your ability to handle load and speed by practicing that direct skill. You don't learn to ride a bike and participate in a 50K bike race on the same day. This requires repetitive skill training and endurance training. The same is true for building processing speed in the brain. First, you must know your starting place and then you must train to boost the skill. Getting a starting place can be done quite easily both formally and informally. Formally, getting a measure of your processing speed can be done by getting a cognitive assessment done by LearningRx either digitally or in person, or you can go to a psychologist to have formal testing/diagnostics. Informally, you can measure your own basal skill by a couple of simple tasks. One such task is card sorting. Take a deck of cards and sort into black/red as quickly as you can and time yourself. Another quick measure is by using a listing technique such as naming as many colors as you can in one minute. Then try with another category like naming all the foods you can think of or as many people as you can name. Take an average of these to get your basal, and then divide that by 12. That's how many items your basal level of rapid naming recall in five seconds is to start. That's the number you want to beat by naming things in five seconds.

So now, we have our starting point, let's race against time.

Name five fruits that start with P. ***** Now what's the third one you said.

Count backwards from 100 by 3s....97, 94, 91....faster now....

Now that I've gotten you started, continue working those skills with games like Five Second Rule, Scattergories, Scrabble Slam and apps like Chain of Thought… those are just a few fun ones to add. Enjoy the learning experience and keep challenging your brain. For a super fun time, come join us at LearningRx with our private workouts. We have group events once a month and private individualized sessions of brain boosting power training daily. Give us a call to get your game on!

LearningRx of Shreveport-Bossier 318.797.8523 Come join us in the fun! *Lola*

> You don't learn to ride a bike and participate in a 50K bike race on the same day.

GRIT
-AND-
WITS

The importance of instilling both in your child.

WRITTEN BY
DONESA WALKER, M.ED,
OWNER OF LEARNINGRX
OF SHREVEPORT-BOSSIER

What's the difference in a Formula One car and a regular sportscar? SPEED is the obvious answer, but there are other differences as well. The sportscar can operate in this "normal" world, while the Formula One car requires a certain pavement type because of its tires. It requires a special gas and a special treatment. It has a different measure of endurance and a different measure of expectancy. While it is fun to watch and fun to drive, it doesn't have the same function as a regular sportscar. Surprised that we are discussing sportscars? It's a parable. An illustration. Everyone is not designed to be a Formula One car with all of the special bells and whistles. Changes have to be made to those cars to make them street legal and able to function on our roads. So, what if we compare the Formula One car to the brilliant children/students we have who are having a hard time in the "normal" environment of life as we know it? School is a challenge and shouldn't be with their IQ or social situations are a disaster and shouldn't be with their EQ (that's emotional intelligence for those that haven't heard of it). How do kids nowadays function in this fast-paced world whether they are a regular sportscar, a souped up version, or a Formula One racing car?

Recently, a great TED Talk video surfaced all over social media from a former educator turned University of Pennsylvania psychologist. Angela Duckworth presented her research that the best indicator is not just IQ but rather a special blend of persistence and passion she calls "GRIT." This research is not new, University of Connecticut psychologist Joseph Renzuli, who is the Director of the National Research Center on the Gifted and Talented, conducted a very famous study and concluded that "task commitment" together with ability and creativity was an essential component of giftedness. Duckworth

even has a survey you can take to determine your GRIT as www.sasupenn. qualtrics.com (a score of 7 is perfect and if you get that, well, it will say that your score cannot be determined as they have not enough data with that score level - ask me how I know?). My son, who is in 3rd year of college at 18 and has a very high IQ, scored a 3.33 and was grittier than 70% of the population. So, what does this mean? Not a brag but rather an interesting look as what makes a person successful and how do we groom this "GRIT" or "task commitment" in our children and in ourselves, no matter what skills sets are today.

First of all, I think we can all agree that today we are more self-aware in our society than ever before. After all, this is the age of social media and posting everything you do from every dirty diaper changed to the foods we eat and the places we go. We are told to support this and abstain from this by every media outlet in the world both fake and real. If we don't post it, our families or friends will, so might as well beat them to the punch. In this world of fanfare, how do we raise successful, productive children who have a good view of themselves especially if they have a learning difference or are gifted? The truth is that we must give our kids both opportunity for success and opportunity for failure. That's right. It's not a typo. Our kids must learn that not everything turns out the first time we touch it and that sometimes being the smartest doesn't mean being the best. Smart is something I spend a lot of time doing as I am a brain trainer/teacher by trade. I often have friends who say "you are the smartest person that I know" and while I really do appreciate that

they think this, I want to say "Am I the happiest?" The answer to that is that I am extremely happy but my IQ didn't bring me that (not bragging about IQ as I really am not the smartest person I know for sure). Happiness to me is more than success, more than IQ and more than any other measure out there… happiness is knowing who you are and being content with that which includes constantly working to better yourself while enjoying the journey. Happiness is a mindset.

I agree somewhat with Mark Erlandson, who is the parent of a gifted student and a successful person in his own right, when he writes in his article "Is Grit More Important than Intelligence?: How to Make Sure our Children Have Both," that developing character in a child is the most important thing that leads to success. He quotes Paul Tough from "How Children Succeed: Grit, Curiosity, and the Hidden Power of Character," saying that failure from overcoming adversity is what produces character and that is ultimately what leads to true long-term success. Character comes from the small things such as training a child to send thank you notes for receiving gifts at special occasions beginning with that very first birthday present! Character comes from sitting on the bench watching everyone else play when you didn't get to practice on time. Character comes from experiencing the highs/lows of personal triumphs and failures whether in sports, academics, extra-curricular or relationships. I know that when a child struggles, it is important to get them the help they need whether that is brain training at LearningRx, a personal fitness

> "The truth is that we must give our kids both opportunity for SUCCESS and opportunity for FAILURE"

instructor, a personal sports coach or trainer or even a counselor. I know that just being there as a parent even when you are clueless on how to help them with their current attitude or mindset except through prayer and constant nagging is important. If we shield our kids from the hard things in life, we do them a true disservice. Allow them to experience them both in the good and the bad. Quit allowing the blaming of the society and people groups around you and get out to experience the world. Mindset, according to Carol Dweck, a Stanford University psychology professor, can change things drastically. In her study, students that knew or were told that intelligence is malleable and trainable earned better grades during the next two years than those that thought IQ was fixed no matter how high their IQ was! (She has a survey too that you can take at www.mindsetonline.com).

Finally, balance. Wow, this is more important than most realize. I recently was listening to a mom sharing her daughter's schedule and I thought, I wonder when the child just breathes? Remember that balance so you can just breathe is so important. Everything being done doesn't make a perfect life. I remember my super-mom days when I tried to juggle school, work, church, extra-curricular and being a wife and mom, and I felt tired and defeated even on a "successful" day. Then I discovered "balance" instead of "juggling." Juggling meant that I always had the feeling that something was slipping and that I was failing at being the perfect mom… I was trying to be the Formula One car in the "normal" world and the race was kicking my behind. Balance meant I learned to change tires figuratively, although I really can do it literally, too! I learned that I have to let some things go and not stress about it. Our children really need this lesson in

this highly competitive world of trying to out creative the next person with our HOCO invites. Balance means training our kids that sometimes it's okay to say "I just can't right now," which doesn't mean that I won't try. It's okay to give up an activity causing an undue burden unless it is building character or affecting a better outcome for the child long-term. It is OK even if you are the lead dancer to put dance on hold this year to get academic help. It is OK if you have a 168 IQ to struggle with math problems… you just need to get the right help to train you in math. It is OK to make changes to your life… in fact, you will likely be all the better for it. Remember Life is a journey and sometimes that journey is the minivan loaded with screaming kids because it is naptime and sometimes that journey is the award-winning race in the Formula One car…. The trick is to enjoy the trip and to stay in the moments of the journey! Lola

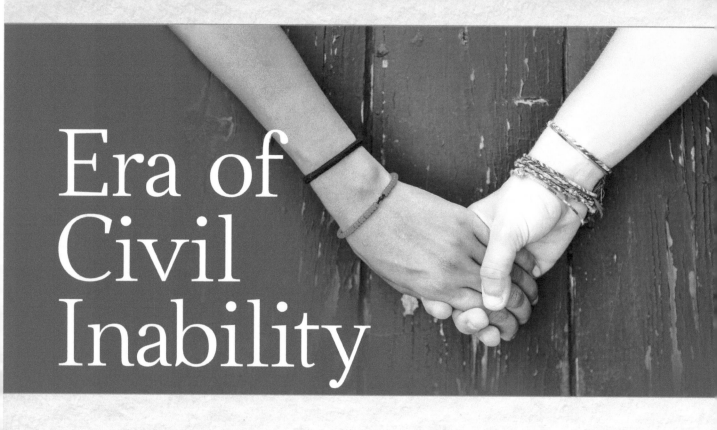

Era of Civil Inability

WRITTEN BY DONESA
WALKER, M.ED,
OWNER OF
LEARNINGRX OF
SHREVEPORT-BOSSIER

Welcome to the era of lost civility.

The definition of civility is formal politeness and courtesy in behavior or speech. The error of our society in allowing this loss of civility is impacting our whole culture and way of life. The change in this starts with the parent and can move back to civility with a few steps in the right direction. And frankly, this is the season to turn over this new leaf.

Why is this so important? Children and adults all over the USA are demonstrating behaviors that at best are poor and at worst are shocking and heart breaking, most of which are the result of a lack of respect, which is the first victim of civil inability. So, how do we turn the tide and begin to breathe the air of civility back into our culture? It starts with good parenting and a firm hand as instructed through scripture. Our cultural foundation is now cracking due to a lack of small steps that technology has allowed and many of us have fostered.

Let's start with a question. How many Christmas cards did you receive or send? Now, how many thank-you cards for your Christmas presents have you sent? I have polled about 15 families at this point and none of them testify to having sent either. Why is this? Culture and technology have allowed this lost step - it is time consuming and doesn't seem to have immediate value. However, I disagree with this philosophy and the research actually backs me up with this.

"Civility does not mean the mere outward gentleness of speech cultivated for the occasion, but an inborn gentleness and desire to do the opponent good." – Mahatma Gandhi

When I first searched for the term incivility, imagine my surprise that there is an actual group that studies this! A quick synopsis of their "Civility in America VII: The State of Civility" is below:

Although Americans recognize a shortage of civility in their daily lives, they easily agree on what it is and what it means to them. To kick off our survey each year, we ask respondents to write in what civility means to them personally. Top responses focus primarily on being nice or polite to others (29%) and treating others with respect (17%). Examples of civility definitions provided by respondents include:

"Being civil — thoughtful, kind, sympathetic, able to get along with others, understanding in thought and word."

"Respect and honor people as you would like to be treated."

"Observing the rules of social etiquette, even when one disagrees."

"Treating one another with mutual respect."

"The act of being civil. Remaining polite, even if you don't necessarily want to."

"Tolerating people and things you don't like for the sake of peace within a group."

To ensure that all respondents completed the survey with a mutual understanding of civility, we presented this definition once they had written in their own: "By civility, we mean polite and respectful conduct and expression." "Civility in America VII" shows that incivility continues to be pervasive in American life. However, Americans are willing to take some actions to prevent incivility from becoming further normalized. We suggest the following calls to action, based on our findings from this year's study:

Let's take the "civility challenge." Three-quarters of us report that we would be willing to personally set a good civility example. We should take that challenge on. As Americans, we collectively recognize we have a civility problem, even a crisis, on our hands. Yet, while we agree on what civility means, we don't see ourselves or even the people close to us as part of the problem. Each of us should take a closer look at our actions on a daily basis and evaluate if our own behavior may be having a deleterious impact on others.

Refrain from posting or sharing uncivil material online. While this is intuitive and perhaps simplistic, half of all incivility is encountered in search engines and on social media. What may seem civil to the poster/sharer, may be considered very uncivil to others. Through sharing and liking, our content often gets seen by people who aren't our direct social media contacts. If we want to set an example of civility, we need to be thoughtful about the implications of not just our real-life actions but our online actions as well.

Leaders of workplaces can do more to root out incivility. Our research shows that working in uncivil environments has an adverse impact on the bottom line and the personal lives of employees. Most Americans report working in civilized environments. Organizations should evaluate their workplace civility levels, understand which factors drive incivility experiences or perceptions — such as anger, low morale and isolation — and correct the behavior.

Find common ground. The political polarization in America that has only become worse applies to civility as well. Whereas some people think that our public squares are better because citizens say whatever is on our minds, others believe our public squares have become breeding places for hate and lies. If Americans could become more accepting of arguments on both sides of the political spectrum and listen more to each other, common ground could be rediscovered and our civility crisis eased.

All of this is well and good but I suggest that we take it a step further. Children learn from their examples and if their examples are demonstrating to them that it is all about them then they will begin to believe that and act on that. I have often been asked by a parent or grandparent why their child has turned into an "ungrateful brat." My answer is the same each time, "What are you doing to TRAIN your child/grandchild not to be self-centered?" We live in a world of iPhone and social media where the world is commenting on what you are doing and how well it is done which encourages an "all about me" approach.

Let's try something new. What if we encouraged our children give up something daily for another person? A seat while waiting at a restaurant or an item that they no longer care about even though they just got it for Christmas. What if we made sure that our children were taught to send thank-you notes for Christmas even if they didn't like the present? I was grateful to get a pair of underwear and an orange from my grandparents as that is all they could afford. Imagine my surprise every time my child sends a thank you note to someone that it gets commented on because it is so rare - this is a small step to changing our air of civility.

When I was watching SharkTank the other night - talk about uncivil - I saw a product go for millions that flabbergasted me! It was called HATER and it is an app to match couples by what they HATE instead of what they like. WOW! Just WOW! We have gotten to the point that hating is more important than liking or loving. Choices, folks! So here is my Civility Challenge to you, should you choose to accept it! - - - - - ➤

Written by
DONESA WALKER, LEARNINGR

TIPS

that will make this the best LEAP year ever
and help with every test to come, too!

I t's that time of year again when the dreaded high-stakes LEAP testing looms over schools across the state. The mandatory LEAP2025, or Louisiana Educational Assessment Program, is designed to provide insight into how well our schools are instilling grade-level skills and knowledge, but for families, it's often a high-pressure time of stress and dread, especially with testing changing constantly and pass/fail attached.

Obviously the best way to get a good LEAP score is to know the material and be able to recall and use it in a timely manner. Aside from that, there are things students and parents can do to make taking the LEAP and other tests a little easier.

> *Perhaps the most important thing you can do to help your child take better LEAPs is a different kind of test –*
>
> ## A COGNITIVE SKILLS TEST...
>
> *Just one weak skill can keep your child from doing well on LEAP and school in general."*

Parents can start by going over these tips with their students:

1. **Pay close attention to all the directions.** Don't just assume you'll know how to fill in the blank or when to stop. Practice bubbling in answers.

2. **Use all the time.** If you finish the test and have time left over, review your work. Make sure you've answered all the questions, shown your work and used proper punctuation.

3. **Skip the hard questions and move on.** Come back to them if you have time.

4. **Finish the test!** If you're running out of time, quickly scan what remains and take your best guess on multiple choice questions. You'll have a better chance of getting it right than if you write down nothing at all.

5. **Breathe deeply!** Stress and shallow breathing can cause each other. If you breathe more than 15 times per minute your brain gets 40 percent less oxygen than needed for normal functioning. This oxygen deprivation is often why kids who should do well on tests, simply don't. To reduce stress, and increase oxygen levels, take a deep breath, briefly hold it and slowly let it out. Repeat five times.

Parents can also help their child take a great LEAP with these:

6. **Make sure they get a good night's sleep.** Studies show a sleepy brain works harder and accomplishes less. Sleep deprivation decreases attentiveness, response time, memory and performance.

7. **Feed them well.** The right combination of foods can help them get that good night's sleep and power up their brain. "Carbohydrates are associated with producing serotonin which can be a calming influence," says Shreveport registered dietician and counselor Emily Cascio. "So an extra serving of complex carbs, such as whole grains, at dinner or before bed can help initiate sleep. Protein is associated with making them more alert – making it an essential part of a pre-test breakfast."

8. **Water them.** Even slight dehydration can cause a physical shrinkage of the brain and impair concentration and thinking.

9. **Encourage them.** Studies show kids do better work when praised for their effort, not for their grades or results. Instead of focusing on getting top scores, encourage them to work their hardest and try their best and the scores will follow.

10. **Practice.** The Louisiana Department of Education's Testing Resource Center at **LouisiananBelieves.com** is loaded with materials to help kids with the various LEAP tests. Don't overdo it! After all, the LEAP is designed to test what your children know, not what they can cram in with test prep materials. But simply running through a previous LEAP may reduce some of the stress because they'll know what's coming.

Perhaps the most important thing you can do to help your child take better LEAPs is a different kind of test – *a cognitive skills test.* This will assess their underlying mental skills like attention, memory, logic and reasoning, processing speed and visual and auditory processing. Just one weak skill can keep your child from doing well on LEAP and school in general. After the assessment pinpoints your child's cognitive strengths and weaknesses, you can focus on the best ways to make weak skills stronger, which will lead to better LEAPs and a lifetime of easier learning and testing. *Lola*

DONESA WALKER, LEARNINGRX

Longtime educator, reading coordinator and dyslexia specialist Donesa Walker, is the Executive Director and Owner of LearningRx Shreveport/Bossier City. LearningRx specializes in identifying weak cognitive skills and strengthening them through intense, one-on-one, game-like brain training. For a free two-page guide with more test-taking tips, email Donesa at d.walker@learningrx.net.

DISCOMBOBULATED:

▶ *Surviving in the Smart but Distracted World of Technology & High Stress/Pace*

Spring is here, spring fever is in the air and summer is truly on its way. So much is happening with graduations, getting ready for college, or even getting those babies and young ones set up for an amazing summer experience with camps and vacations ahead.

The stress/pace of this high-tech happening world surrounds our minds and it honestly gets super overwhelming sometimes, especially for those who already struggle in this area. The saying goes "when the cat's away, the mice will play." In other words, when there is not a strict demand of order, chaos reigns. This is true in the brain also and the skill most associated with this CEO position is called the Executive Function. Just as we all have different irises in our eyes and different face shapes, and unique fingerprints, so our brains vary from person to person. In fact, identical twins often have the same iris print, fingerprint and DNA/blood, but I have never seen/heard of the same exact brain function and in fact, of all the twin sets we have tested, none have tested exactly the same. This matters because some brains are incredibly creative and others are extremely organized. Some are easy to work with and others need to learn how to work with their own brain.

Executive Function (EF) is a set of skills that includes cognitive flexibility, and this has been determined to be one of the top ten skills necessary to compete in the job market by 2020. EF includes time management, emotional and behavioral control (EQ), initiative, attention, working memory and persistence (GRIT). So how do we measure these things in life and how do we approach the training of these skills to their upmost efficiency?

Many books are written on this very topic, but we are going to touch on just a few. First, a little biology. The prefrontal cortex, which is the area where most EF takes place, is still developing in young people up to their mid-twenties ... necessary to know before you blame everything on the Millennials! New skills on average can take around twenty-eight days/repetitions to become a habit, but those who struggle with Executive Function Disorder often take three times as long to develop these habits necessary to effective employment and successful academic performance.

As a mother of young men, I often see the struggle with managing this brain growth

WRITTEN BY DONESA WALKER, M.ED, OWNER OF LEARNINGRX OF SHREVEPORT-BOSSIER

and steering it in the right direction. As a professional brain trainer, I often see "the apple doesn't fall far from the tree." Know what I mean? While many of these skills were still developing in us when our parents "trained" us, we did not have the technological affluence to add to the battle. Recent research and informational data loads have demonstrated that the youth brain in development is highly sensitive to the reward center receiving dopamine (the feel-good hormone) dumps just by touching their phones. Wow, and I thought a little chocolate was bad!

Since the young, developing brain is constantly rewarded via technology for being off task and inattentive, the battle is harder than we realized, and this applies to adult brains, too. *Lola*

So, what to do? Here is a list of tips to restructure and train the brain into a better state of EF.

1. **Perform a self-assessment.** Be honest with yourself and write down the areas of struggle. Grade yourself, then also have at least one someone else (a friend, colleague, parent, spouse) "grade" you in the following areas 1-5, with 1 being weak skill and 5 being high skill (self-understanding, organizational skill, time management ability, emotional/behavioral control, flexibility, initiative, attention, memory, persistence.)

2. **Create a growth mindset** by getting rid of all negative talk, especially self-talk. Research and scripture has taught us that this leads to a negative mindset and little is accomplished from that. Restate negative thoughts positively.

3. **Accountability.** Get an accountability partner who will "justly" not "rudely" hold you accountable for your successes and your failures.

4. **Change your perspective.** The saying that "attitude determine altitude" is truth. If you are constantly seeking your own way and never looking objectively at the situation, then you will not make change. If at first, you don't succeed, then try, try again!

5. **Reach out to professionals who can help.** If you struggle with cognitive flexibility, attention, organizational skills or memory, reach out to a professional brain trainer like LearningRx or a local doctor who specializes in these areas. If you struggle with emotional/behavioral control, get with a counselor, psychologist, or behavioral therapist and seek help. If time management is an issue, there are lots of apps out to there to help you become better at this. If you struggle with initiative and persistence, partner with someone, even a parent or friend, to help you learn these skills.

Procrastination leads to failure.
Get up and get going. Start now!

RATE YOURSELF ON A SCALE OF 1-5:

_____ **Self-understanding**
(I am truly aware of my strengths and weaknesses)

_____ **Organizational skill**
(I can manage and organize my space/life/work details well)

_____ **Time management ability**
(I am prompt and timely in my performance/attendance to expectations from others)

_____ **Emotional/behavioral control**
(I do not let things around me overwhelm me to the point that I lose control)

_____ **Flexibility**
(I can roll with the changes/punches life sends my way)

_____ **Initiative**
(I can self-start, and I do not procrastinate to avoid people/situations)

_____ **Attention Selective**
(I can focus and ignore distractions)

_____ **Sustained**
(I can pay attention to even boring things for a long length of time)

_____ **Divided**
(I can multitask and not lose place of what I was doing)

_____ **Memory Short term**
(I can remember what I am told and follow multi-step directions well)

_____ **Long term**
(I can recall important information and details of events and happenings for a sustained period of time)

_____ **Persistence**
(I do not give up and I will keep trying no matter how hard the situation is)

*****Recommended self-intervention:** The Executive Functioning Workbook for Teens by Sharon A. Hansen.
Call LearningRx about a 30-hour seminar they are offering for these skills this summer.

Do Not Go Gentle Into That Great Night
Combatting Memory Loss

WRITTEN BY DONESA WALKER, M.ED, OWNER OF LEARNINGRX OF SHREVEPORT-BOSSIER

One of the greatest fears humans face today is the loss of our mental capabilities, and yet it is happening more and more at an alarming rate. Some of the questions I hear often is "Is this Alzheimer's?" How do you know if it is age related cognitive decline known as "oldtimers", early onset dementia, or Alzheimer's Disease? What can I do to combat this memory loss?

Dementia is a syndrome and not a disease. Dementia is an umbrella term which encompasses a group of symptoms that affects mental cognitive tasks such as memory and reasoning. Dementia can occur due to a variety of things, one of which is Alzheimer's disease. The causes of the rate of large memory losses are still up for debate depending on who you talk to but one thing we know from research findings is that a low sugar, low wheat diet such as a Mediterranean Diet is helpful in slowing the progression of the disease and that deliberate brain training can help with this also. One of the most invigorating and helpful physical exercises is gardening.

The biggest factor with all of these is Quality of Life (QOL) measures which affect not only the individual but also the caregivers and associated family members. Research has indicated that having professionals involved in the daily care/activity of those suffering actually increases the QOL of all involved. Interventions that assist in maintaining mobility, physical activity and mental/cognitive function actually make a difference in longevity and QOL. Focused cognitive training with a professional brain trainer actually had more long-lasting results than that of any computer intervention or mild stimulus interventions according to the most recent research. The Alzheimer's related brain changes can start as early as age 40 and factors that influence this plaque building brain disease include high levels of inflammation such as those caused by repeated head trauma as well as low dopamine levels.

Again, this research is ongoing and there is not a definitive test available at this point that indicates Alzheimer's with certainty. Rather, it is a set of symptoms. So what are the best things to do? Be aware of head trauma and get intervention to address this early on, be cognizant of dietary factors that affect dopamine levels, and do preventative interventions such as brain training throughout life. *Lola*

10 Alzheimer's Early Warning Signs *from the Alzheimer's Association*		"OldTimers" *or normal forgetfulness*
	MEMORY LOSS that disrupts daily life-asking the same question over and over, forgetting important dates/times, increasingly having to rely on family members as memory aids.	Forgetting names/appointments but then remembering them later
	HAVING DIFFICULTY WORKING WITH NUMBERS, paying monthly bills, difficulty concentrating and taking a lot longer to do simple tasks.	Making careless errors on these things but catching or correcting later
	DIFFICULTY COMPLETING NORMAL EVERYDAY TASKS that are familiar like how to drive to a certain location or even how to get from one room in the house to another, or remembering rules to a game played for years.	Needing some help with new technology
	CONFUSION WITH TIME OR PLACE, forgetting where you are or understanding passage of time.	Confused about day of the week but suddenly remembering or knowing that you forgot
	TROUBLE UNDERSTANDING VISUAL IMAGES and spatial relationships such as difficulty reading, determining color, taste, smell, judging distances, etc.	Vision changes
	NEW PROBLEMS WITH SPEAKING WORDS or writing them, struggling to find words in a conversation, repeating themselves a lot, calling things by unusual names that describe such as Hand clock for watch.	Trouble finding the right word immediately but later getting it
	MISPLACING THINGS and losing ability to retrace steps such as having no clue thing is missing or having no recollection of last place they were-occurs more frequently over time. Confusing placement on items-Putting keys in fridge and milk in pantry	Misplacing things from time to time and having to retrace steps to find them
	DECREASED OR POOR JUDGEMENT when dealing with money, grooming, keeping themselves clean, and other decision making.	Trusting others too easily and making a bad decision once in a while
	WITHDRAWAL from work/social activity and unrationalized fear of people/situations such as forgetting how to do a favorite hobby or avoiding crowds of people especially things they enjoyed in past.	Feeling weary of work, family, social situations or crowds for long periods
	CHANGES IN MOOD or personality such as becoming anxious, fearful, easily upset in both familiar and new places.	Being set in ways and getting irritated with changes in routines

The biggest DOs are...

✔DO get a cognitive test for yourself and your loved ones early on so that you will have a baseline to measure against should these concerns arise. There are lots of professionals who offer this at a reasonable cost in the immediate area including LearningRx.

✔DO be deliberate about doing intervention activities such as family brain game nights & brain training games/activities. For a free sampler, contact LearningRx.

✔DO be deliberate about your dietary and exercise regimen. Many healthcare professionals out there now have lifestyle health coaching that address these factors.

✔DO a follow up cognitive test if any family member has any type of hit to the head...as this can lead to further difficulties down the road especially if your child is involved in sports known for head trauma such as football, hockey, lacrosse, soccer, baseball and even cheerleading or tumbling. Most insurance companies cover this type of testing to some extent.

✔DO engage a professional cognitive skills trainer such as those at LearningRx if you or a family member struggles with memory loss due to any of the aforementioned factors.

✔DO see a qualified healthcare professional such as neurologist or psychologist if you find any of the above factors are affecting your QOL or that of a loved one.

Is it TRUE?

How to Survive the Uncertainty of the Post-Truth Era

BY DONESA WALKER

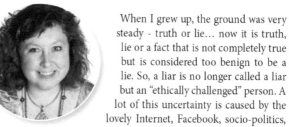

Have you ever heard of quicksand? I have, but I have never personally experienced it although I have seen it used as a plot changer in lots of movies/TV shows, as well as in many books. Quicksand is a mire that a person gets stuck in and the more he tries to get out of it, the worse his situation gets. He must anchor to something outside the quicksand in order to pull himself free or all is lost as this muck slowly sucks him to his death even as he stays unmoving. This is the situation that our current world is in. And this is the mire that we must train to survive.

Imagine my surprise when a few months back on a Sunday morning at church, the pastor of a local church I attended stated that we were in a post-truth era... What in the world is that? I had never heard of such and frankly immediately rejected the very idea.... Wait, that is exactly what it is... immediate lack of trust for what we hear/see/experience from previously respected resources.... How did we get here in this quicksand, and how do we get ourselves out?

Post-truth was announced in 2016 as Oxford Dictionaries' International Word of the Year "as it is the word more than any other that reflected this past year in language." Post-truth is defined as *"relating to or denoting circumstances in which objective facts are less influential in sharing public opinion than appeals to emotion and personal belief."* The fancy word for all the study and research around this is **Agnotology**, or the study of culturally induced ignorance or doubt. So, what has really happened, quicksand...

When I grew up, the ground was very steady - truth or lie... now it is truth, lie or a fact that is not completely true but is considered too benign to be a lie. So, a liar is no longer called a liar but an "ethically challenged" person. A lot of this uncertainty is caused by the lovely Internet, Facebook, socio-politics, etc. Truth is not defined as a certain moral principle anymore but rather a fact I can choose to accept or decline. Sure, many blogs, magazines, newspaper articles blame the middle-class voters for this as they elected Trump and they declare him the epitome of this era; however, I don't want to discuss politics but rather how this era is affecting our local businesses, our children's future and our current relationships with others.

Consciousness is defined as pure awareness governed by truth. Jesus said, *"I am The Truth, The Way, The Life."* The anchor that must be used to get us out of this quicksand of post-truth is just this.... Truth and yet so many are afraid to hear it as it does not agree with their agenda, wants, and beliefs that it is immediately rejected. How do you combat this to succeed? Constant steadiness of truth. Truth isn't popular. I especially do not like it when it is against me personally... truth like "it is cancer" can be undeniable (although even that is debatable now), but how it is treated is no longer status quo or easily accepted.

Doctors, teachers, business leaders and even pastors who were once respected as authorities in their fields are now questioned and second guessed and to tell the truth, this isn't always a bad thing as it does require the brain to examine and think deeper. Challenging current mindsets of

individuals, groups, business models and professionals isn't always popular nor is it bad, but neither is sticking only your hand into quicksand.... It only becomes dangerous when you immerse yourself in it without looking where you are going. So, what determines the right/wrong amount of examining and questioning? Truth... the anchor... the thing that pulls you out because it is unsteady and unwavering... upbringing .... moral character... Biblical principles.... Never before have all of these things come so heavily under fire.

Navigating this post-truth era of quicksand is a challenge in all areas of life, but there are a few things anchored in truth that will hold steady whether in personal/professional relationships, business practices, or even online interactions. I love the poster using **THINK** as an acronym **T-True? H-Helpful? I-Inspirational? N-Necessary, K-Kind...** If these simple principles guided our relationships well in the past, can they not guide them well today? I like the words written thousands of years ago in Philippians 4:8 *"Whatsoever things are true, honest, just, pure, lovely, and of good report, if there be any virtues or any praise, think on these things."* These are the anchors. The first in both of these is **TRUTH**. If the very foundation of who you are is being questioned, the truth of how you were raised, the truth of your beliefs, the truth of all that you know is shaken to the core, what do you hold to? **I anchor in Jesus.** Many even question who He is. But I know Him. And THAT is the key.

Relationship. Here is the basic truth that will get you out of the quicksand of this life. **Get to KNOW the people, businesses, persons you trust...** Everyone makes mistakes and all of us dip toes, fingers, hands, arms, and sometimes even sit on the bank of the quicksand of life, but our anchors are the people and relationships around us. As a small business owner, I want my families who interact with us to KNOW me. Because in knowing me, they will trust my heart. They will know that I truly will do all in my power to help them. You see, even the man completely drowning head under in the quicksand can be rescued with a strong anchored relationship. I especially love the scene in *"The Princess Bride"* where Buttercup is swallowed whole by the lightning quicksand but her love, Wesley, grabs a thick vine anchored to a huge tree and jumps in after her headfirst and pulls himself and her to safety by trusting in the vine. This again goes to scripture where Jesus says, *"I am the vine and you are the branches, he that believe in me shall have life and have it abundantly."*

Find your anchor. Hold on tight, especially if you decide to walk without looking where you are going. Establish close relationships around you so that when you misstep, those around you will grab hold of the vine and jump in to rescue you. Surviving the quicksand of this era is knowing the truth and not allowing yourself to be wavered. Here's to you and your relationships built deep in trust. *Lola*

ATTITUDE
of GRATITUDE

How gratitude can rewire your brain

BY DONESA WALKER, M.ED. OWNER OF
LEARNINGRX OF SHREVEPORT-BOSSIER

"ATTITUDE TAKES YOU TO HIGHER ALTITUDES" is a favorite saying of mine that indicates my feelings on being grateful. In fact, not only is this my opinion, but there is irrefutable evidence that being grateful actually rewires the brain and makes the overall health of individuals very helpful. The benefits of gratefulness include: reduced pain, healthier lifestyle, better sleep, stress relief, decreased depression, reduced anxiety and increased energy.

In a 2009 National Institutes of Health study, researchers found that the hypothalamus activates when we feel/act grateful and/or display acts of kindness. These acts flood our brain with dopamine, which gives us a natural "high" in our reward center, making us want to perpetuate the acts again. In addition, a 2003 study states that counting blessings versus burdens, 10 percent of patients reported less pain after writing in a gratitude journal.

Not only does gratitude help us learn to act with more kindness, but it can reduce pain in our bodies and even help us get more rest. A recent study on sleep concluded that patients who said prayers or had thankful thoughts before going to bed actually fell asleep more quickly and had better quality of sleep. So instead of counting sheep, count blessings.

Another great benefit of sleep is stress relief and reduced anxiety and these also are benefits of gratefulness. A 2007 study of hypertension patients demonstrated that patients experienced a significant decrease in systolic blood pressure by simply using a gratitude journal. An additional 1998 study showed that 23 percent of heart patients decreased cortisol levels and 80 percent had increased heart function just by doing the same type of journal.

So not only the brain is benefiting, but also healthcare and overall wellbeing is benefiting. In 2005, a study of clients struggling with depression actually showed an increase in neural modulation and decreased depression by writing letters of thankfulness, and in a follow-up study in 2012, a whole slew of patients benefited from reduced anxiety by writing thank-you notes. Who wouldn't want the added benefits of increased energy, lengthened lifespan, increased strength, as well as a healthier, more optimistic and more relaxed life?

Approach this season of thankfulness and giving with an attitude of gratitude and reap the benefits. Here are a few ways to be deliberate with the attitude of gratitude as the season of thankfulness and giving approaches. *Lola*

Take time to **SAY THANK YOU** in verbal, text, email, and written thank-you notes.

COUNT BLESSINGS. Get a blessings box or container and when the day is rough, read back the blessings previously recorded.

Keep a **GRATITUDE JOURNAL,** which forces the brain to think in terms of gratefulness daily and then rewards the brain with dopamine to celebrate.

Do deliberate **ACTS OF KINDNESS** and record them with a smile.

POST WORDS OF GRATITUDE and uplifting acts of kindness to Facebook or other social media sites.

Surround your workplace/home with **WORDS OF GRATEFULNESS AND POSITIVE AFFIRMATIONS**.

Seek out **POSITIVE PEOPLE** to be around. Season the grumpy ones with kind words.

PRAY/MEDITATE daily.

Explore ways to **EXPRESS THANKFULNESS** to others.

Share affirmative thoughts with others and **SMILE!**

> "Who wouldn't want the added benefits of increased energy, lengthened lifespan, increased strength, as well as a healthier, more optimistic and more relaxed life?"

beendoggled:

Putting the Right Foot Forward, *or is it the Left?*

BY DONESA WALKER, M.ED.
OWNER OF LEARNINGRX OF
SHREVEPORT-BOSSIER

tarting a child off on the right foot is often a challenge and leads parents on a merry chase to find the correct preschool offering or setting that will give the child the best opportunity to make it big in the world. But what all parents want most is a happy, well-adjusted child who will flourish and not struggle. The demands of the curricula today are most difficult for many parents to wrap their heads around, much less to assist their student in the learning process, especially in the math field where the methods of teaching and performing math have changed drastically from their own experiences in the classroom. Gone are the days of math facts recitation repeatedly on a daily basis and here are the times of multiple ways to get to a solution and show me each way. The process has become more important than the answer and this is hard for many to grasp. Here are a few thoughts to help guide parents in this new competitive world of choosing the right path for your littles.

Cognitive development is the upmost importance in a child's development of skills that will follow him/her all the way through the school system. Unfortunately, many parents do not know to get a cognitive assessment done or even where or when to start this process. When to get this assessment done is before starting school, but it is never too late. Adults can benefit from knowing their own cognitive strengths and weaknesses so they too can work on enhancing their own skill sets. Where to get this assessment is from a respected resource like a local psychologist, school specialist/diagnostician or a reputed resource such as LearningRx. Many preschools even partner with some of these resources to get screenings or offer discounts to these facilities. For example, getting a child's vision/hearing checked is essential to making sure that the student has the ability to see and hear the information being delivered, but what if the brain cannot process the

information at the speed of delivery? This makes the student struggle to keep up with the others in the class and ultimately fall behind. Or what if the memory is not as strong as it should be because the apple didn't fall far from the tree? Then the child struggles to remember what the teacher has told them or to follow multi-step directions when orally given…so how do these things get addressed? Knowing the strengths helps to continue to build on these and knowing the weaknesses allows for the intervention necessary to get the child off to the right start. After getting the results, then the fun begins.

Cognitive intervention/exercise is much like that of the physical exercise and many times even involves using body movement as this connection is crucial in the brain. Gross body movement includes large muscle groups and fine motor movements include things like handwriting. If a child struggles with motor movements, an Occupational Therapist or Physical Therapist can assist with assessing and treating this difficulty just like a Speech Therapist can assist with assessing and treating speech difficulty such as delayed language or difficulty with forming certain sounds. Cognitive Therapy falls into two categories: behavioral and foundational. A Cognitive Behavioral Therapist assesses and treats the behavior much like a counselor but with intensive intervention such as play therapy and other techniques to help address behavioral concerns while a Cognitive Trainer such as those at LearningRx actually exercises the brain's ability to use memory, processing speed, attentional issues and logic. Cognitive exercise is something we all do to some extent because we use our thinking skills daily but when an area is weak it is used less and thus never strengthens. It is the purpose of cognitive exercise to deliberately work these weak skills until they become stronger. As a result, IQ is boosted and the student becomes a better learner at any age. IQ is simply the sum average of all of our thinking skills and the stronger these skills are, the better the IQ. Neuroplasticity means that the brain is malleable and that it can be trained, which in turn boosts the sum average of the skills (IQ). **

"games and toys that are difficult and challenge the child are beneficial and can boost great thinking skills."

One of the most incredible ways to work on cognitive skills is simply through games. Games of all types including limited technological games have value but it is the interaction with the adult that increases the vocabulary and trains the child to think. Learning to cook well means that one must practice the cooking and not just watch and read a recipe; learning to play the piano means that one must practice doing so in order to become a master at it… the same is true with thinking skills. In order to become a master at thinking and processing lots of new processes, thoughts and data, one must practice doing so. Games and toys that are difficult and challenge the child are beneficial and can boost great thinking skills. Local toy store owner Sarah Toups at LearningExpress Toys prides herself on carrying the best thinking games and toys to challenge the brain and her staff is eager to assist anyone in the purchase of games that will target specific skills that the child needs to work on. In addition, there are many free games and activities both online and homemade that can be beneficial to boosting a child's cognitive function.

LearningRx and LearningExpress Toys are partnering to offer a special Mommy & Me classes in February aimed at teaching family members to use these games and activities to boost cognitive function in the littles.** Gymboree and many of the other local facilities such as Bricks for Kids, Code Ninjas, music/dance/karate/gymnastics and so many more also offer classes that work on different parts of whole body/brain connections. The main point is to be deliberate. Do not wait and do be purposeful in starting your child off right whether it is the left foot or the right. And SchoolHouse Rocks still has benefits so put some music on that teaches a few facts and dance the night away with your preschooler, for after all, the parent is the best toy/learning activity that a child can have, and that includes the cardboard box with which to make imaginary places, for it is the imagination that takes us places through incredible reading and playing together.

**For more on this incredible, ground breaking research, please look at all the research available online via LearningRx website at *www.learningrx.com/research*. For more on class offerings or assessments, call the LearningRx office at 318.797.8523, email us at *Shreveport.la@learningrx.net* or simply stop by at 8856 Youree Drive Suite D. *Lola*

USE IT OR LOSE IT
Brain Fitness for Full Function

BY DONESA WALKER, M.ED.
OWNER OF LEARNINGRX
OF SHREVEPORT-BOSSIER

Brain Awareness. *What is it?* I am aware that I have a brain and that I use it occasionally, but what am I supposed to be aware of in particular in the special month of time? Brain Awareness is a special time set up to recognize the higher-order thinking processes called cognitive function that make us human and help us rise above the animal population. Most of the tips I give you here are truly no brainers as they are things that you already know and some of you already do, so this will just reaffirm that you are doing well and you are human! Some of us can benefit from these reminders as we get too busy to process all that we should and often fail to follow through. So, for those of you wanting to check on your progress toward being aware that you are human and have a brain, *here are a few reminders of the things you should be doing each and every day as you celebrate Brain Awareness Month.*

BREAK A SWEAT. An overall healthy lifestyle which includes regular exercise is believed to boost brain health and to lower the risk of dementia. Partner up for a daily walk or hire a personal trainer to challenge you to new heights as a local gym. There are so many opportunities to get daily exercise. Did you know that gardening was one of the leading ways to exercise the brain and the body while getting the benefit of the rich foods that your body needs at that same time? Relaxing the body afterwards with an Epsom salt bath can also give the body some needed magnesium as

nutritional aid while calming those tired muscles. Get in touch with local fitness experts or join a local gym as there are a myriad of offerings in our area.

FUEL THE BRAIN. Keep a hydrated body and brain. Dehydration can lead to short-term memory loss as well as a myriad of other issues in the body that ultimately affect the brain. The rule of water is to drink half your body weight in ounces of water daily just to maintain full function. *Did you know that your brain uses 80% of your daily water intake to power it?* So how much fuel are you giving your brain? Save the trees, use your brain instead of sticky notes or recording the memos...to increase the brain power, fuel it with water.

FEED THE BRAIN. The brain's brain is the gut, so choosing good foods that are high in nutrition for the brain is a smart choice. The old adage you are what you eat holds true as more than 85% of Americans are magnesium deficient and this is only one mineral that is necessary to the brain health as well as gut health. There are lots of vitamins and supplements as well as shortcuts out there but truly there is nothing better than plain nutritionally rich foods. Your brain prefers colored foods because these bright-colored foods are rich in the vitamins and minerals that your brain needs to perform at full capacity. Fish oils and omega

vitamins are good for you, but it is so much better to get all of this from eating the right foods. For help on getting in on healthy lifestyle and nutritional choices, contact a lifestyle doctor or specialist in our area by calling *Wellspring 365 at 318.655.1259*.

CHALLENGE YOUR BRAIN. Break a mental sweat. Doing what is easy for your brain does not give it enough challenge to grown and change so do what is difficult. Hire a personal brain trainer to challenge you to new heights. If you find that logic games and activities are challenging for you, do more of this. If puzzles are easy, try Sudoku instead. Get a personal fitness checkup with local experts. These assessments can be had for a small price with long-term benefits. Make your brain health a priority. *LearningRx of Shreveport-Bossier* is your local brain fitness expert and you should contact them at *318.797.8523* for an assessment or personal brain training.

PROTECT YOUR HEAD. Remember that a hit to the head can lead to traumatic brain injury, which has a permanent effect on your thought processes as well as everything else that your brain controls. Wear helmets, seat belts and other protective gear when traveling or playing sports. Be proactive about brain health and particular about your head. For more information on this, contact *ThinkFirst of the ArkLaTex at 318.226.0066.*

MAINTAIN STRONG SOCIAL CONNECTIONS. One of the leading causes of suicide is lack of social connections or feeling bereft without a go-to person to contact. Shreveport-Bossier is blessed to have so many resources to stay involved in our community. One way to stay connected and to give back is to volunteer your time. There are so many places that would love to have a volunteer at all ages; one is to contact *Laura Alderman at StepForward 318.404.1755* as she can plug you in to great opportunities to form lasting social connections to the children in our community or contact *Volunteers of America* locally as they have many ways for you to get connected.

KEEP A HEALTHY SOUL. Prayer and meditation can lead to a better outlook. Get involved with a local church that can help you find ways to nourish your soul. Get a daily devotional book or read the Bible. Spend time focusing on the things outside your normal hustle and bustle by enjoying the beautiful nature gardens or lakes we have around the area.

DESTRESS YOUR LIFE. Put away the high-demand projects and things that eat your time and leave you with nothing but negative words and feelings. Do not engage in social media that dries you out but focus on the things that bring you joy and light. If your job is stressing you out, find an outlet to destress during that day such as time away mentally doing something you enjoy during breaks or plan time away to destress. Get a massage, read a good book, use scented oils, or simply paint your nails to feel more alive.

GIVE OUT OF NOTHING. This is the number one way to boost brain health. Give a smile, give a kind word or a thought to someone else. The brain actually is rewarded every time you give. Give to those in greater need than you. Give time. Give gifts. Give money. Pay for the food of the person behind you in the drive through or prepare an extra dish of food and drop it off at a senior center as a gift to someone in need. Go through your pantry and take cans of food to the food pantry. There are so many ways to give and you can even combine this with your social time and gets both benefits for your brain. *Contact the Community Foundation at cfnla.org.* Send a card to a soldier or to a resident of a care facility. Go sit with someone in need at the *Cancer Center* or drive someone to their doctor appointments.

SHARE YOUR LIFE. Not enough is said about this but sharing your life stories and experiences is incredibly good for the brain and boosts our self-esteem. If you do not know someone to share with or feel like you want to keep things private, contact a local counselor or therapist. These folks are there for a reason and are so willing to listen. Share your thoughts in a journal or a blog, even Facebook if you feel open enough to do so. Sharing is a necessary part of life and can greatly benefit brain health. Share with those around you because by doing so you open connections in your brain and form new neural pathways. Your schema is developed more fully, and you get deeper connections to the world around you. Share your joys and your pains, share your sorrows and your wins. Share your good times and your bad because after all this is what makes us human. *Lola*

3.141592 ...

FINDING BEAUTY IN THE HIDDEN PLACES

Understanding the Joys of Parenthood While Celebrating the Pain

BY DONESA WALKER, M.ED.

Parenting is described as the hardest job with the least amount of recompense and yet it is also the most fulfilling job with the greatest rewards and deepest sorrows. I'm feeling very reflective these days as my boys are both moving on in their lives and that means change. Moving from being Mommy to Mother. Last year as this process became a reality for me, through deep pain, I wrote the poem "This Mother's Hurting Heart".

That pain was deep and awe inspiring but it also caused me to examine a role I had always dreamed of but never fully understood. The Role of Motherhood. This role is not for the weak nor is it for the male counterpart despite what society wishes to say to the contrary because we are specifically designed and tasked for this role from creation. I know this is not a popular thought nor is it the current trend but it is the truth. Motherhood is a role for women because it requires a certain understanding of who we are as women. The feminist movement has had some good and some bad to it. It has helped

and harmed the female role in our world. You see women were never meant to be equal to men but rather to do all the things that men cannot. God specifically chose to design a woman differently from the man. From dust, He created man...yes, the rhyme of how boys are made which says ...of dirt, snails and puppy dog tails, well, the dirt part is true...and from bone, he made woman. Not just any bone, but the rib bone. The bone which is closest to the heart for love and under the arm for protection. Man was made in God's image and woman was made to be a helpmate for him to accomplish the big challenges that God had given him. Sugar, spice and everything nice is the things girls are made up of so that rhyme goes but the truth is that sugar can be too much sometimes and give you tummy aches and the spice, well, some of us are just spicier than others... the everything nice...well, this is a lesson that needs teaching to a few! The point is celebrating women doesn't mean putting them into a

box nor is it trying to make them exactly like men. Women as mothers are not only life bearers to populate our earth but women are life bearers from creation. We are meant to give life to others through our words, deeds, and actions even if we never give birth or mother others in the physical sense. When trying to achieve any other purpose, a woman is found desperately searching for the person she is to become.

A mother isn't a role that happens only because we gave birth. A mother is a role we choose to fulfill. I said I always dreamed of being a mother and even in school and college people laughingly called me "Momma Donesa" because I was always trying to "mother" people. Mother isn't a role I will ever grow out of or change. New memories will be made and new roles in life will be played. I will always be a mother. But the time of the children being dependent on me has shifted and this is bittersweet. Recently, I said as much to my mom and she said she knew, and for me to remember she lost three kids at once...that's because my sister and I traveled off to college shortly after the murder of my brother in 1989. I can only imagine now the pain she felt and how bereft

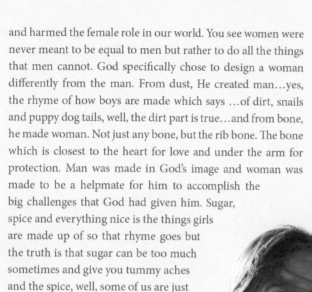

THIS MOTHER'S HURTING HEART

WHO KNEW *that when your kids grew up, they grow away?*

WHO KNEW *that the toddlers who once begged for every moment of your time now barely tolerate your presence in search of friends and fame*

WHO KNEW *that those sweet mouths that were once sustained by your breast now break your heart with their careless words not meant to hurt or sting*

WHO KNEW *that those hands that once caressed your necks and twirled your hair now slap at you if you get near as your kisses now embarrass them?*

WHO KNEW *that the feet that once ran in joy to your presence now run away as fast as they can towards others who are much more exciting*

WHO KNEW *that the children who once begged you for more time to read, play & spend with them now see you as a distraction from their lives as they move in a new direction?*

WHO KNEW *that the words I love you from your child's lips would no longer mean you're their only love?*

WHO KNEW *that the hours/days/months/ years of planning birthday parties/special events/etc. that once thrilled their hearts would now become an endurance of epic proportion?*

WHO KNEW *that the endless sleepless nights of crying for you would now become sleepless nights of worry for their future and their safety?*

WHO KNEW *that the scars/pains of childbirth would only begin the scars/ pains inflicted unintentionally by those same children?*

WHO KNEW *that those nightly cherished hugs/kisses might be your last?*

WHO KNEW *that your morals/advice and wisdom so carefully shared would be ignored with disdain for a time until they learn them themselves?*

Only Another Mother. And her advice: Cherish these moments because those days of sweetness are but a few and soon you too will touch the pictures in memory poignantly wishing for those days long past....

- Donesa Walker

the emotions. My mother is my best friend, confidante, and example, as well as being my hero. Never did I imagine that I was her biggest blessing and her biggest heartache at the same time. You see, that's the role of mother. Finding the beauty in the hidden places. Finding the diamonds under the coal. Finding the gold amid the dirt. Finding the rainbows despite the storm. This is the depth of Motherhood.

I hear tell by those around that being a grandparent is super cool and so much better than parenting but I find that hard to believe. I loved being Mommy. It was my dream and I continue to live it fully. It is time to embrace new dreams and

time to fill those days with being Mom, Mother, Grandmom, Friend, Sister, Mother-In-Law, and many more.

So, a loving salute to all moms out there whether you are a mom in the making, a mom on loan, a mommy in the battlefields of toddlerhood, a mom swinging the teen years, a mother in law, a mother in age, a mother of none or a mother of many. Motherhood is a blessed time of life that starts from the moment you are born a woman to the end of your days. For today, I lean on the wisdom my Father taught me...You are always a mother for you are the mother of the woman you will become. *Lola*

OUT *of the* POOL
and Back to
SCHOOL

School readiness at all ages

Getting off the summer slide and getting the brain ready for the academic prowess of school is an important part of July. Celebrating the July 4th holiday, then beginning to purchase school clothes, backpacks and supplies consumes our time and minds. But backing away from the brain drain of summer means more than just gearing up with supplies. It means that the brain must be made ready once again for a fantastic year of learning. Here are a few tips to avoid the dread of another school year and instead get the brain in gear for a great start to a fantastic year.

BY DONESA WALKER, M.ED. OWNER OF LEARNINGRX AND BRAIN TRAIN LEARNING SOLUTIONS

41

1 Cognitive skills & fitness

Working memory is the biggest predictor of school success. Recent research has shown us that in order for a student to have the largest success in academic skills, the students must have cognitive flexibility, which requires adequate working memory. What kind of memory? Working memory... that is the amount of memory your brain has to keep multiple thought processes occurring somewhat simultaneously. I say somewhat because the brain can truly only perform one thing at a time, but the efficiency of task switching relies on the short-term memory and the working memory. When working memory is in high demand but not enough of it available, the brain simply cannot remember multiple steps or directions and confusion or complete shutdown occurs. There are several ways to enhance this type of memory, but each of these requires deliberate intervention. One, a person can enroll in a cognitive fitness intervention program such as that offered at LearningRx, which personalizes the fitness workouts to the needs of the client. Two, a person can do online games such as Brain apps and games with a purposeful and meaningful approach spending time each day doing these. Three, a person can choose to play memory games such as board games like 5 Second Rule or Scattergories daily. Fourth, one can choose to do recall activities, such as remembering what is in the refrigerator or on a particular shelf. Knowing the strength or weakness of this skill and deliberately enhancing it can make all the difference to a year of success. Being cognitively fit means that the student struggles less to learn even if the instruction is hard to understand. Cognitive fitness can be the key to opening up doors to the students' futures.

2 Grit & fortitude

Grit is one of the biggest determiners of completion of a task or goal. Grit means that the person perseveres no matter what is thrown their way and this is a trained skill. The difference in grit and fortitude is important to recognize. Fortitude is defined as mental or emotional strength that enables courage in the face of adversity while grit is defined as firmness of mind, invincible spirit, courage or fearlessness. Fortitude comes naturally to some and others struggle in the face of adversity, but grit can give one fortitude. As brain trainers at LearningRx, one of the biggest factors is training the students to persevere under the pressure, learning to manage stress by letting the pressure become a source of fortitude rather than a weight. Ways to enhance this in your child is simply letting them become bored and learning to do something with that. Let them struggle through a situation or hard place by encouraging them that they can do it if they will persevere and that you are there with them. Reminding them that at 211 degrees, water is just really hot. But one degree more of effort and the water boils, which means it takes off into the air as steam...it transcends the current uncomfortable place to become more.

3 Mindset & motivation

Growth mindset is the most powerful source of motivation as it allows the person to see the potential of what can be. Encouraging growth mindset is an everyday activity. It requires the restati ng of the I can't to the I can if I give it another try and if that fails, then one more time. One of my students came in saying this is impossible and he learned quickly that there is no such thing. Eating an elephant starts with one bite at a time. He quickly changed to saying this is hard but it isn't impossible and this has helped him strive this past year to be on the honor roll despite his struggles in learning in the past. Understanding that change comes because I make it happen rather than change comes and takes me along for the ride is the key to unlocking growth mindset. There is a terrific resource for this at BigLifeJournal.com. The Resilience Packet or the Growth Mindset packets are well worth the investment for your child or grandchild.

4 Nutrition & hydration

Never can enough be said about hydration for the brain and nutrition for the body which affect the brain. 85% of Americans do not get enough magnesium into their diet to keep their brain function at capacity of growth and 80% of Americans hydrate incorrectly. Each morning, before anything else, every child should have a glass of water. The brain and body become dehydrated overnight. How can the brain function without fuel? Put a bottle of water on your child's nightstand and teach them to drink it as soon as they wake up. This will help with short-term memory. Get a baggie of mixed nuts and super fruits to snack on throughout the day, which will help with the magnesium benefits and end the day with an Epsom salt bath especially for those in sports as this will help with muscle cramping too.

5 Sleep & rest

There is a huge difference in sleep and rest. Sleep should be restful but not all rest is sleep. Sleep should be 8-10 hours for the teen to child ratio. Too many Americans especially young ones are suffering with too little sleep due to technology. No streaming videos, gaming, TV or tablets at least 1 hour prior to bed! The brain cannot fall into proper REM sleep until it processes all of the information seen and taken in so if your child is going to sleep to TV or videos then their sleep pattern is being interrupted. Remember to limit the daily intake of technology to 10 minutes times the age of the child... that's correct...none for those under 1 and that toddler should not be walking around with a tablet or consuming TV hours at a time. Rest is critical for the brain and this is important to the overall health. Rest means no stimulating brain activity and that includes vegging out to TV. The brain needs to rest at least 15 minutes per hour in order to function well. So that means that for each hour of activity, the brain needs a few minutes to decompress...I know that schools don't often provide this time but teach your child to find it when they can. A moment of prayer or meditation can have the same effect, so teach them deep breathing and restful mindfulness.

For now, it's a few more weeks until school, so take the time to incorporate these habits above into a cognitive fitness lifestyle. Take some time to rest by that pool and do some brain games. Enjoy the times with friends and family. Snack on some nuts and take a hot salt bath. Go get a massage and enjoy some random, boring down time so that your brain can come to the best year ever! *Lola*

Q&A: THE LAUNCHING OF
The BrainTrain Learning Solutions

Q Tell us a little about you.

A I am a lifelong educator passionate about the learning process for all people. I believe learning should be fun, engaging and full of experiences. I worked in the public school system for over 20 years in addition to several years in administration in charter/private school settings and within the homeschool community for over 10 years. Most recently, I have worked in the cognitive training industry for the last 11 years here in the Shreveport-Bossier area as the owner/director of LearningRx of Shreveport-Bossier. Through these experiences, I have seen the need for a wide variety of services and so the birth of The Brain Train Educational Services has been a long time in the making. I am a wife and a mother of two wonderful sons. I am active in my church and happy to be a contributing part of this community.

Q What was the motivation to open this new avenue? I mean you have been so successful here for the last 11 years doing brain training at LearningRx so why the change/added services and why now?

A Frankly, need. So many clients have come to me with a wide variety of need from an advocate for their dyslexic child to a coordinator of special services for parents struggling with memory to needing someone to advise them on homeschooling curriculum or needing assistance with finding the right mix of things for an ADHD child. I am still here to offer brain training as this is a very important piece of what I have been doing but I no longer am limited to only that as a resource. The need for more has grown as more and more people of all ages need to address their cognitive function in different manners. Technology and changes to the way we educate have introduced new avenues of learning as well as new challenges and I want to be able to embrace all the pillars of learning and provide a more robust service to our community. I also recognize that some services are very costly and I want to be able to reach out to more with a variety of price points and product offerings that will fit more in line with the budget and time constraints of our community.

Q *What will the new services look like and how do people know what they need?*

A That is exactly why I am opening this more robust offering. Most people struggling with learning don't know where to start and many people struggle with where to turn for advice. Does my child need tutoring or brain training? Should I do meds or try a natural route and which natural route? What is the first step when I am starting to struggle with my memory or I have a parent who is beginning to struggle? Should I choose public, private or homeschool and which school is right for my child? It is so confusing for so many people and there is a constant demand or barrage of information that causes an overwhelming overload and people are scared they are being directed one way or another and not sure it is the right way. I can tell you that as a parent, it is undoubtedly the hardest job ever and then as a daughter with parents who have had health concerns that have affected cognitive function, that is hard too. Even my own recent medical issues put this top of mind that it is super important to have resources and to know who those resources are in the community. In essence, I am choosing to open this side of business as an economic, cost efficient resource provider to the community to help direct them to the different options we have so they can make better choices. Many of the offerings we have in Shreveport-Bossier are not even available in other parts of our state at all.

Q *Do you not think that you will be a little biased in your offerings, I mean, after all, your other business of LearningRx will be offering some of the services.*

A That is true. It is hard not to be biased in truth in some ways but I am a pretty forthright person and anyone who knows me will tell you that I will tell you the truth even if it hurts a little. I definitely do not know all, but I plan to be able to offer a wide variety of services with the focus on cognitive function obviously as well as to be a community resource of other services available in our community.

Q *What are the exact services that you will be offering now?*

Some of the offerings will be:

1. *Cost effective/affordable homework help as homework in this day/age is often very complicated and we are so busy that it is hard to get it done. Especially projects like science fair.*

2. *Instructional specialist advising services so that parents/students can come to one place to look at various options for schooling from preschool through college.*

3. *Educational testing/review so that parents can get a true unbiased measure of where their child is and can take these results to other qualified professionals if needed or can use results to make curriculum decisions.*

4. *Homeschool, private school and local public school shopping guides…we will have a menu of what each school has to offer and hopefully even can help with scheduling tours or have dates for open houses, etc.*

5. *For the adult, we will have menus of local services that can partner to help with different needs such as knowing who to go to at which step of concern as well as getting back into school options, resources, etc.*

6. *Brain training options through LearningRx are still available as well. But we will also have other specialists we can offer a menu for such as psychologists, psychiatrists, counseling, speech, physical therapy, occupational therapy, etc.*

The primary reason for all of this is to be a one stop place where people can go to see what local resources are there for their learning needs at various ages without just having to pick luck of the draw or waste time searching on the internet & cold calling only to get frustrated with what is/is not available.

Q *When will these services be available to the public?*

A We are building up the menu of offerings and doing all the research necessary to be able to offer a full menu by May but we are beginning with the homework/project help now. It is only $15 for ½ hour of help which is super reasonable and we look forward to being able to help a lot of frazzled parents get some peace at the end of this school year. We will even have a listing of summer camps/VBS and other offerings soon so people can start shopping for those too. As a mom, this was so hard to try to find which things to involve my child in and where to sign up and how to know all the stuff…guidance counseling on these things is so important. Knowing that Shreveport-Bossier has incredible offerings and many times people just don't know about them, I hope to shine a light on many of these and open doors to new opportunities in our area. *Lola*

ERASING THE STIGMAS OF DYSLEXIA & ADHD:

JUST THE FACTS *without all the* HYPE

BY DONESA WALKER, M.ED.
OWNER OF LEARNINGRX
AND BRAIN TRAIN LEARNING
SOLUTIONS

J ust hearing the labels ADHD or Dyslexia for some gives them chills and anxiety, but the truth is that everyone has cognitive skill differences and the knowing is half the battle. Cognitive skills are the thinking skills we use every day to make sense of the world around us and they control everything we do from breathing to memory. When there is an inefficiency in these skills, we often end up with labels such as ADHD or Dyslexia just like when the body inefficiently manages our blood sugar, we end up with the label of diabetes. This does not determine who we are nor who we are capable of becoming.

The core cognitive skills that affect the overall efficiency of learning are long-term and short-term memory, processing speed, visual/auditory processing, logic and reasoning, and executive function. Executive function

Each day we are training our brains and ourselves to be THE BEST person we can become NO MATTER how old you are.

is the skill that is essentially the CEO of your brain. It helps you to control the overall management of the other skills and things like senses which can lead to sensory overload or time management issues as well as ADHD or Autism. Finding the weakness in this skill can be as easy as identifying which of the six components of executive function you struggle with: organization, focusing and task shifting, regulation/sustaining effort and processing speed, managing emotions, utilizing working memory and recall, or self-monitoring and self-control. Dr. Thomas E. Brown calls these the Executive Function Impairment of ADHD: Activation, Focus, Effort, Emotion, Memory and Action. Identifying where the struggle is and working on that skill can make all the difference in the world especially for those who struggle with ADHD.

Logic and reasoning impacts math skills, test-taking skills, comprehension skills, understanding abstract concepts and impulse control. Addressing this skill through rigorous training can give the person the ability to handle tasks with more thinking before they act as well as improving test taking and math/comprehension skills. Processing speed is the hardest of the skills to address as it requires the speeding up or slowing down of the thought processes and requires the person to learn to listen to his/her own thoughts and to manage this skill through exercise. This is often paired with meditation or breathing exercise as this is an important aspect to learning to manage anxiety.

Visual and auditory processing are very important as these skills impact all of the learning experience and the way that information is encoded to memory. The visual-spatial sketchpad is the tool that we use to hold things in working memory to work on them much like our screen on our computer holds what we are currently working on while on the computer. Learning to utilize this sketchpad correctly such as learning to hold information there or when to discard this information can be the difference in following multi-step directions correctly and being a good listener. It can also impact the way we read as we can create a visual movie of all the different things we read about on this brain screen. Pairing it with the auditory processor, which manipulates the sounds we hear into words, and words into meaning as well as the letters we see into sounds we can blend into words that have meaning can be the difference in enjoying the reading process or making it a laborious task to be dreaded.

All of these skills add up to different strengths and weaknesses, for example, typically a dysphonetic dyslexic person can struggle with not only memory issues with the code of the English language, but also the understanding of the sounds that letters/words make and the processing speed of the brain. This can be really confusing as there are about 13 different ways we make the sound A in our language and only one is by the letter A at the beginning of the sentence -- how about EIGH for example? That's why a sentence like "The bandage is wound around the wound" can be so confusing!

There are many different types of attention issues and many different types of dyslexia, dysgraphia, dyscalculia, etc. But none of these defines a person anymore than someone with a heart condition is defined by that. Remember the next time that you see someone struggling with learning or behavior that inefficiencies do not define us. We define them by how we refine them. Struggling with learning issues isn't a way of life, it is something that can be trained. No one stays the same. Each day we are training our brains and ourselves to be the best person we can become no matter how old you are.

Take a step today to be the best person you can be. Partner with a local brain trainer and overcome some of the challenges you face to continue towards the best you. LearningRx and The Brain Train Learning Solutions are happy to partner with you to direct you to the resources in our community that can assist you with being the best person you can be and helping you to discover the greatness within you or your children, grandchildren, spouse, etc. Most of all remember to cherish those around you for who they are no matter what their differences.

Gifts of
a Lifetime

The *Spirit of Giving* is a gift.

That "give the shirt off your back" kind of generosity is something only a few people truly possess and yet it is a trait that can be given to others simply in the training of it.

When I was young, my mother told me that JOY was spelled Jesus-Others-You, meaning that you put God first, then others, then yourself last. In today's society we often get this backwards and yet it is so important in raising our own that we continue to reach out to those around us so they might be blessed. It is in this spirit that I share my personal story of our family and our blessings we have each year.

Wanting to be in the right attitude at Christmas time, I struggled on how to do this with my little ones as going to the rescue mission or volunteering service was so hard when they were little. We decided that each year we would select an experience for us to spend time with each other and that should include the blessings of other people within our realm. As little guys, our boys were fascinated with the fire fighters, calling them "fighter fighters." They always wanted to bless the fire fighters as the engine house was close, and we took cookies or brownies over often and talked to them and got on the trucks, even had them come out for a fire fighter-themed birthday party. In thinking of how much my littles loved this, we decided to bless not only the fire fighters but to spend the next year collecting and setting aside for a gift to give at Christmas to bless others who were "burned out" of their home. I simply got a small fire engine and attached a gallon Ziplock baggie to it, and all of our extra change and ones made it into that baggie for that year as well as some of the "extras" we had around the house becoming a small pile of blessings. Then just at Christmas time, we made some reindeer cookies and took them along with the monies and "extras" to the firehouse to be a blessing to the next family in need. This was the start of a really wonderful concept because my kids couldn't wait to see who was next.

On Christmas Eve, from the time the kids were little forward, we have had a present under the tree and it was the first present we opened. It was simply a small box that has a name inside it of whom we planned to save for and bless the following year. My boys are grown now and we still travel or take an experience together and yes, we had presents under the tree, but we always try to understand that it is not the number of gifts nor the price of the gift nor even if it is valuable to you or something you want but rather, it is the heart of the giver that is in that package so you carefully unwrap and you think of the value of that heart. Taking the time to write thank you to those who blessed you with their heart at Christmas is as simple as turning over the paper that the package was wrapped in and saying thank you while signing your name or drawing a picture. The gift of gratitude and the gift of giving unto others comes from the act of giving and thankfulness. Over the years, we have been blessed with so much and we in turn choose to bless others who are not as blessed through the various ministries and opportunities that are out there. Generosity of spirit is a gift and it can be shared and it can be trained.

When I was asked to share this piece of my story with you, I thought of how to do so without it seeming to be snotty or prideful because that is not what it is about nor who I am at all. The point of Christmas is a celebration of the ultimate gift we all were given in the form of a tiny baby who was the Christ in human form. The shepherds came to worship him and the wise men brought him gifts (yes, I know this was actually much later but tradition…). It is in this that we tried to stay in our thoughts. Three gifts to symbolize the gifts of the wise men. Three gifts only per person under the tree and of course, the Santa surprise when they were very little… but, it was and still is the best to open that small box on

BY DONESA WALKER, M.ED.
OWNER OF LEARNINGRX AND BRAIN TRAIN LEARNING SOLUTIONS

48

Christmas Eve and know that the ultimate gift is in the blessing of those around you. This should be a daily calling and yes, we do that too, but it is special to know that you are working and saving to bless others as Christ has blessed you with the gift of life. In the world of fraud and cheats, people who lie and steal to get from others in so many ways, it is still so refreshing to be able to bless someone or a ministry with a small gift of thoughtfulness and the JOY that comes from that cannot be had in other way. Some of my friends ask me who are you giving to this year and I always say, to the place that God has laid upon my heart.

If you are in need of a place to start your giving, simply choose an outreach or a person in your scope of influence. LearningRx and The BrainTrain Learning Solutions gives to the homeless shelters every year. You are welcome to join us in the giving. We are accepting new blankets, pillows, and hygiene items such as small toiletries, soaps, shampoos, toothpaste, etc., and these will be taken to the homeless in the week prior to Christmas. If you are in need of a list of places to save and donate to, there are so many ministries from Angel Tree to Roy's Kids, nursing homes to the homeless. Scripture says the needy you have with you always. It is not always will you have the opportunity to bless them so take the opportunity to teach your littles this year to bless others. There are many in need of so much from those who need brain training and cannot afford it to those who need shoes and clothes. Every penny or gift counts and you can give even when you are the one in need for that is how it comes back to you. If you cannot give financially or in gifts, give your time. There are many in need of a simple listening ear or to have a book read to them. *Lola*

DYSLEXIA:
THE SUPERHERO RETURNS

The jumble of letters and symbols wasn't getting any better no matter how long he looked at it. It didn't seem to matter how strong the medicine was that his doctor prescribed, his mind still couldn't focus on these archaic symbols and understand their meaning so once again, he gave up with a headache and a sigh of frustration. It was now an everyday occurrence and he was tired of fighting to try. Kevin* begin to try to think back to his whole school career and when was the last time he truly felt successful in school. He still loved building and he remembered his kindergarten class…that was it… the last time he felt happy at school and excited about learning.

Kevin watched his Kindergarten teacher, Ms. Baker. She was so pretty and smart. He wanted to be just like her when he grew up, well, really, just like his daddy, but smart like Ms. Baker. Ms. Baker was making some pretty markings on the board and wanted him to make them on his paper too. One of them looked just like a bridge tunnel. He liked to build bridge tunnels. Then she handed out papers to color of the bridge tunnel. She called it something else, a fancy name like N, but he was confused about that. For now, he just wanted to think about the bridge. He really liked building and he could make this bridge really cool with his colors, so he began to really enjoy that. He thought about Batman fighting the Rock on the bridge tunnel while he was coloring and suddenly, he heard his name being called. The class was going out to recess and Ms. Baker wanted his paper, but he wasn't finished making it pretty for her, so he stuffed it into his desk. He would give it to her later after lunch when he had time to finish the pretty bridge.

Kevin never finished his bridge tunnel coloring. In fact, it wasn't long after that his mother came to visit the school and talk to Ms. Baker. Ms. Baker told his mother that Kevin had trouble with attention and couldn't complete his work and focus in class, so his mother took him to the doctor, and he got some medicine. The problem was that the medicine did not make the jumbled symbols and letters make sense either. Kevin wasn't sure what the medicine was supposed to do, but mostly, it made him tired and he just didn't feel like doing too much anymore.

Thinking back to that day, Kevin wonders why it was so easy for the other kids and why he has struggled so much. Kevin has been on medicine since Kindergarten and he still cannot read. He is in special classes to read and he had even memorized some words, enough that most people think he reads just fine but to Kevin, words and sounds related to symbols on a page are still a mystery.

This is one story of a dyslexic child. Dyslexia is not a disease nor really a dysfunction as some may define it but rather an inefficiency of the brain to decode the symbols called letters when grouped together into sounds and to code those same groupings into words. There are many different types of dyslexia and most are overlooked. It is obvious when students struggle with sounds and reading that there is a reading problem and that is one reason the National Center for Learning Disabilities has determined that 1 in every 5 children struggle with a learning disability. The scary thing is that it is higher than that, as 2 in 5 children struggle with reading specifically and only one of these will be correctly diagnosed and treated. More often than not, children are incorrectly diagnosed, and

proper treatment is rarely applied as in a typical school system, struggling students continue to grow to hate learning.

I often am asked why so many who come to my learning center are dyslexic or struggle with reading. It is because their parents have finally found a place to make a difference in their child's life and have chosen to take that step. What makes brain training different than the other interventions of the educational world specific to dyslexia? The one to one intervention. The sequence of the skills delivered simultaneously. The addressing of all the underlying skills that cause dyslexia and not just the auditory weaknesses addressed by an interventionist or speech therapist in a group setting. Training the brain to tune into the important aspects of learning. Showing the brain how to code these sounds into a pattern of language. The intensity of the sessions that allow the brain to automatically discover that neurons that fire together, wire together. The constant feedback from the personal trainer who cares about every aspect in the child's life and can incorporate these frustrating details into the pattern of training for that day, demonstrating to the child how to channel that frustration and anger into a usable skill for learning. This is the difference.

Kevin came to my center in middle school. He had given up on learning and was perpetually beat

BY DONESA WALKER, M.ED.
*OWNER OF LEARNINGRX
AND BRAIN TRAIN
LEARNING SOLUTIONS*

52

down. His parents had tried everything and had given up hope, worrying that Kevin would never be able to stand on his own two feet. He loved sports and he was good at it. He loved drawing and building and her was good at that. He even loved his classmates and teachers, but he was not good at school. Through the years, he had had teachers who really took that extra time and he had struggled on. This year, he was just too tired of it all and he began acting out which got him into further trouble. Kevin came to my center as an undiagnosed dyslexic young teen. He came angry at the world and had given up on learning. Weeks later, I watched Kevin begin to read for himself. At first, it was a struggle, but he now understood the code and he felt confident in himself because he now knew there was a team of willing people supporting him, coaching him, cheering him on. His teachers, his personal brain trainer, the staff at LearningRx, his parents, everyone around him began to see this amazing young man come out of his shell and thrive. As I write this, I just received a text from his mother a few days ago. He is serving our country in the armed forces as an officer. He has graduated college and is married with a child. He is thriving and has chosen to go back to get his Master's degree so after the military, he intends to help others by building the bridges he dreamed of in Kindergarten. *Lola*

This is my why.

LearningRx is a passion for me. It doesn't make me a lot of money nor does it make me a superstar on the scene in the community. All the Kevins out there are my why. For they are my future and I am theirs. The superheroes in this story isn't Batman, but rather the parents who brought their son to LearningRx, Kevin himself for sticking it out until he could get help and all of the brain trainers who give their lives to changing the lives of others. I salute my staff and am grateful for the opportunity to change lives daily. Today as I write this, we celebrate 11 years of changing lives one brain at a time.

name was changed to protect privacy of this particular individual, but this is a true story based on a real client of LearningRx in Shreveport, LA.

8 habits

to better cognitive fitness

Habits are formed when you do something long enough that it becomes ingrained or automatic such as brushing your teeth. The rule of thumb to enforce a habit being only 21 days is a myth. The reality is that researchers from University College London found that the average was closer to 66 days with some individuals succeeding at only 18 days and others (the hard-headed ones) taking almost a full year at 254 days. Unfortunately, breaking a good intention is pretty easy and quick, like some people do this daily, while breaking a bad habit is much harder. According to recent research from Yale University, a bad habit (not an addiction) takes a sustained abstinence of the habit of 90 days to allow the gradual re-engaging of proper decision making and analytical functions in the brain's prefrontal cortex. Addictions on the other hand can be a life-long enemy as recovery can be a daily battle especially with certain drugs and lifestyles. The reality is that this is why so many people have already failed at their new year's goals by the time that you read this article. The goal is to make a new habit by doing it consistently one day at a time for at least two months. So, as you set your sights on the habits of brain health below, pick one or two to follow through on and when that becomes a habit, add another and by this time next year you could have 8 new great brain health habits and a healthier brain, happier life

- **Habit #1:** **Hydration/Nutrition.** Plan to drink ½ your body weight in ounces of water daily and eat lean/green, organic foods, which are rich in nutrients such as magnesium. When you feel stressed, eat some nuts, dark chocolate and drink plenty of fluids. Add spice, reduce wheats and eliminate sugars.

- **Habit #2:** **Read daily for at least 15 minutes.** It doesn't matter whether this is a magazine or a book but reading not flipping through the pictures is the point -- in fact, you are doing your brain good while reading this. When you feel pressure, take a moment to focus on something else by picking up a book/magazine and deep breathing while you read. Perhaps, have a daily scripture reading or chapter in a book if you are not a reader.

- **Habit #3:** **Focus on the blessings that you have each day and spend time in meditation and prayer so that your mind can enrich.** When you feel stressed, journal about it and let the stress flow out into private thoughts that you can pray and meditate on. An attitude of gratitude fuels the brain as it builds up the hope and happiness hormonal levels which leads to a more positive outlook.

- **Habit #4:** **Learn something new and challenging whether this be picking up crocheting or puzzles.** Try something that has been hard for you in the past and keep trying it daily as this help forms new brain connections. When you feel anxious about this, try saying the alphabet backwards! Challenge yourself by partnering with a personal brain trainer who will hold you accountable and push you to learn.

- **Habit #5:** **Socialize with friends and family in a tech free environment at least once daily.** Social connections are important for the brain so spending time tech-free while conversing with others will build the auditory/listening skills and fire up new synaptic connections. If socializing makes you tense, try starting with one friend/family member at a time and make a "date" of it.

- **Habit #6:** **Invest in yourself.** Take time to enjoy something fun, pleasurable and relaxing daily. This can be the good book in the bath with scented candles and bubble bath or it can be a night out with a friend, or even just a piece of indulgent chocolate. It can also be choosing to set aside time to work with a personal fitness trainer or a personal brain trainer which can benefit both the body and the brain. Remember, indulging yourself is not the same as investing in yourself. Do something that leads to a better you and start small with perhaps making an invest in me calendar.

- **Habit #7:** **Create an atmosphere of rest around you.** Sleep properly by making your sleeping environment a healthy place with no TV, electronics, blue lights, etc. Add scents and perhaps an infuser or a room spray that has a relaxing scent like lavender. Strive to reduce your technological intake to a limited amount and cut it off one hour prior to bed. Play soothing music or listen to an audiobook as you drift away. Leave all phones and other WIFI enabled gear out of your sleeping places so that you can dream uninterrupted.

- **Habit #8:** **Set goals for new healthy habits by controlling risky behaviors or habits and breaking out of them.** Choose one habit that is bothering you or irritating those around you who love you and deliberately choose to break that habit whether that be an eating issue, an addiction, or just an annoying habit several others have commented on. While this may be the most difficult of the tasks, it can also be the most rewarding. Choose to be deliberate and substitute the habit with a healthy brain habit such as doing a logic puzzle. If tech addiction is the issue, try going back to a paper/pen world for a while. Partner with a local counselor or therapist who specializes in breaking addiction. Do not let life's cares throw you back into the path of that addiction but get an accountability partner who will hold you to your goals.

BY DONESA WALKER, M.ED.
OWNER OF THE BRAIN TRAIN LEARNING SOLUTIONS AND LEARNINGRX OF SHREVEPORT-BOSSIER

Join the Shreveport-Bossier Community in a Healthy Brain, Healthy Workplace, Healthy Life, Brain Fitness Summit on **March 13** and **14**. For more information or to reach out to someone to partner with you on these goals, reach out to us at **The Brain Train Learning Solutions**. *318.655.3884* or **LearningRx** at *318.797.8523*.

A New Way to Learn *is a* New Way to Grow

BY DONESA WALKER,
M.ED. EDUCATIONAL
SPECIALIST, BOARD CERTIFIED
COGNITIVE SPECIALIST

This obituary doesn't read as one would expect it to read. There is no survived by nor preceded by death in this obituary, for it is the obituary of a way of life. I am not morbid enough to be writing about the death of our society as we know it although that seems to be in the offing. As an educator, I am actually writing about the death of the educational system as we know it and the rebirth of the system it was intended to be originally. This not only applies to education but to so many other fields. We as a society have given our responsibility up to others and have not done our part, and the result is that we have a system that we do not now know or enjoy. I am so fascinated by the American spirit and the ability to rewrite our lives. I am struck by how unbelievably resilient we truly are and that is the key. The anchor to all of that is in whom we trust. The motto on the dollar says, "In God We Trust" and it is that spirit that is unsurmountable. Circumstances may waylay us but yet we still trust.

I have been looking back a lot at history during this time as my son is in college and studying the parallels between this time and the time of the Great Depression. Circumstances are much the same and the parallels are scary, but the spirit of Americans is courageous in both times. What seems to be a really bad and depressing time can be a time of renewal and growth if taken and embraced as Americans are doing.

A little history of educational principles and you will discover that our country was founded on freedoms of religion and education like no other and this founding principle is awaiting rediscovery. When CoVId-19 struck our shores, it was a lack of knowledge about this disease that caused the pandemic and the shutdown of our country resulting in the sudden onslaught of education at home. While some found this an enjoyable experience, many others found it overwhelming and daunting because of the lack of freedom. Many found themselves suddenly chained to a computer for hours upon end through trying to connect their children to educators who suddenly were forced to educate via a portal on Zoom, Google Classroom, etc. For others, the internet was inaccessible, and they struggled to understand packets of worksheets sent by the educators to the home as everyone struggled to find a new normal in this unknown. The freedom came to those who finally gave it up to enjoy educational experience and found the joy of learning with their children. This is what school should be about. It is about learning and the joy of finding this knowledge for oneself through various explorations rather than regurgitated knowledge spit back up on a test. The cause of death of our educational system is not a lack of funds nor a lack of time nor any of the other excuses. My dad always told me that an excuse is a "skin of a reason stuffed with a lie" and this is true. The cause of death is apathy. This is the same cause of death of our society. OK, soap box for a minute here… why are our kids rioting, rebelling, falling for the lies that others tell them? Apathy. Not theirs, ours. History teaches us that apathy about a situation is what leads to downfall of a society. The Holocaust would never have happened except for apathy. But that's a much longer conversation…

Many of you know that my dad and mom as well as a lot of my dad's congregation contracted CoVid-19 and it was not a pretty thing, in fact, some of them are still fighting it. My dad is a miracle that he is alive…but for God and His provision allowing me to educate myself and those caring for him listened. People want to place blame on others around them for so many things and I promise you that is really easy to do. Doctors are not God. Teachers are not God. Law enforcement officers are not God. Every time you try to put someone else in that seat, you will find failures because all of these professionals who do amazing jobs at what they do are simply people who educate themselves and yes, they make mistakes. The reality is that some mistakes cost lives and that is terrible and hard. The reality is that some mistakes cost period…in lives, money, economy, emotions, etc. Why am I saying all of this…to encourage all of us to get off the bus of apathy and into the classroom of life. So many people ask me what curriculum should I use as I homeschool this fall since my kids are not going back to school or in case they cannot go back to school. The answer is simple. What does your child need to know? Do you know this? What is your child's learning ability? Where are their strengths/weaknesses? What skills do they need to develop? I birthed two boys with the same genetics and the same upbringing, but they needed different things in terms of training and education. Can you expect any school to deliver this to your child or any curriculum to do so? The answer is NO!!!

So how do I educate myself and my child on what they should know? Let's look at the basics of knowledge needed and let's start with the foundation of learning.

First and foremost, is learning FUN? It should be fun. Learning should bring joy, and this is a foundational misstep in education. It is not the job of the school to make this happen. The parent holds the responsibility of helping the child to find the approach to learning that brings them excitement and the parent does not give this up by enrolling the child in school. Parents need to take this responsibility back and quit trying to pass it off. I know this is not a popular statement but I promise you that in doing so, you as a parent will experience a freedom that you have never had before and the teachers/school systems that have you on board will be grateful. This does not mean that you go to the school with a list of demands but rather you take responsibility for knowing and understanding the way that your child learns and you provide that type of learning experience for them by accessing the resources that he/she needs in your community and helping the school to know your child in a partnership with the resources.

Community resources such as therapists from cognitive therapy, speech, occupational therapy, physical therapy, counseling, tutoring, etc., are accessible, and some of the best in the nation are here in our community. Many of these function in the school setting as well as privately and many take insurance plans or help you file for reimbursement for those that are out of network. Employing the resources to find the right direction/assistance to give your child the best is the beginning. Then one must make sure that the resources are meeting the needs and that one is continuously monitoring the overall health including the EQ/IQ of the student through achievement to interaction. Admitting when you need help in finding the right resources and getting the help for both yourself and your family is the ultimate key.

Death of a fruit is life to the seed. In other words, all this uncertainty and struggle can be a breath of life to the learning cycle of the struggling learner and can put joy back into learning for those who were struggling. Learning a new way to learn and a new way to grow does not have to be a negative… it can be the beginning.

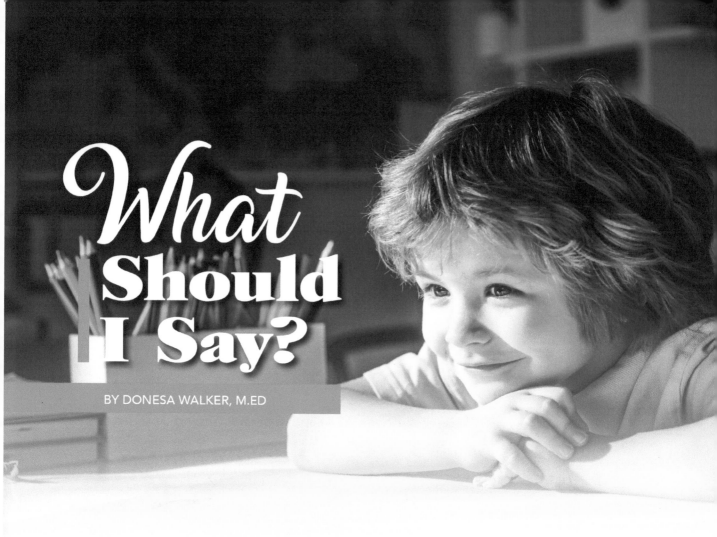

What Should I Say?

BY DONESA WALKER, M.ED

The art of conversation is often difficult with people when it comes to discussing the needs and expectations of a child with learning differences, and in today's society this becomes even harder due to the overwhelming social media presence and the need to present the best side of all of us to the adoring world. It seems that every parent wants the perfect child who has no issues and yet is there really such a thing as a perfect human?

The offense comes when the child appears to be all that is "normal" but struggles with the unseen learning challenge that sneaks upon the parent all of the sudden as the student is leaving for college or heading into high school. Then the blame game starts with parents blaming one another, the school, the teachers, the ex, or even CoVid.

This past week, I struggled with telling a friend of mine that her child had a learning difference that she needed to address. I do this all day long at my office but struggled to find the right words to let her know that it was time to step up and do something now. Why is this so uncomfortable to us as a society? I discovered that this is the unseen and unrecognized "shame" issue. Understand, there is nothing wrong with having

a learning difference or learning struggle and yet we have a really hard time telling others that there is something that needs a helping hand. Is this the same as telling a friend that they have muck on their face or their panty line is showing? No, absolutely not. It is, however, similar to telling someone that they have an emotional/mental issue such as depression or anxiety or discussing that someone needs to intervene in their health like their weight. These are not popular conversations and these are very hard places. What should I say and how do I say it?

First, it has to be a person that allows you to speak into their life. You need to have that relationship already so that speaking into their life is allowed. Second, the best way is not to state it as a fact, but rather to ask leading questions so that they can see what you are trying to say is something that you have observed. Third, it is important that you not use a judgmental tone so that it is clear that you are speaking out of love and not out of malice or spite. Finally, you must offer options or solutions to help them find resources to get to the root of the issue you are concerned about most.

What are the leading questions you should ask? Have

you noticed that your child (use their name) struggles a bit with schoolwork/homework/conversation/etc.? Have you recognized a difference in your child (name please) from their peers or siblings? Have the child's teachers/coaches/or other adult influencers mentioned anything to you about your child's behavior/learning/etc.? Have you had any frustrations in working with your child in homework/schoolwork/remembering directions/etc.? These are just a few of the possible questions you can ask to open the conversation.

Resources: Know what is available and be able to offer these or perhaps you can purchase a gift card to LearningRx where they can get an assessment of the learning skills and a complimentary consultation with a specialist.

Understand that knowing what to say and when to ask these questions is really important. Perfection is not possible for any human but learning easily is and that is the opportunity that you are offering. So, how did my conversation go with my friend? She was already feeling like there was a problem and had wondered why I had not said something! She felt like I as her friend and a specialist would notice if there was something that was going on and I should have said something. So, in short, she was very grateful and now I have the opportunity to bring massive change into that family's life because make no mistake, this affects the whole family and the environment in the home. *Lola*

The MISUNDERSTOOD CHILD

A poem about children with hidden disabilities

by Kathy Winters

I AM THE CHILD that looks healthy and fine. I was born with ten fingers and toes. But something is different, somewhere in my mind, and what it is, nobody knows.

I AM THE CHILD that struggles in school, though they say that i'm perfectly smart. They tell me i'm lazy -- can learn if i try -- but i don't seem to know where to start.

I AM THE CHILD that won't wear the clothes which hurt me or bother my feet. I dread sudden noises, can't handle most smells, and tastes -- there are few foods i'll eat.

I AM THE CHILD that can't catch the ball and runs with an awkward gait. I am the one chosen last on the team and i cringe as i stand there and wait.

I AM THE CHILD with whom no one will play -- the one that gets bullied and teased. I try to fit in and i want to be liked, but nothing i do seems to please.

I AM THE CHILD that tantrums and freaks over things that seem petty and trite. You'll never know how i panic inside, when i'm lost in my anger and fright.

I AM THE CHILD that fidgets and squirms though i'm told to sit still and be good. Do you think that i choose to be out of control? Don't you know that i would if i could?

I AM THE CHILD with the broken heart though i act like i don't really care. Perhaps there's a reason god made me this way -- some message he sent me to share.

For I AM THE CHILD that needs to be loved and accepted and valued too.

I AM THE CHILD that is misunderstood.

I AM DIFFERENT - but look just like you.

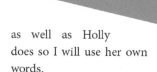

family

The Gift of a Lifetime

BY DONESA WALKER, M.ED. BCCS,
OWNER OF LEARNINGRX AND BRAIN
TRAIN LEARNING SOLUTIONS

Taylor June

Amazing mom Holly is no stranger to telling her story and I lived it with her through her Facebook feed for a while and recently through our interconnection at LearningRx. I first met Holly through Cosse & Silmon as she does their marketing and we cross market sometimes as well as refer to each other. Her contagious laughter and sweet smile make her an instant hit with anyone. Taylor June was the baby girl of her heart if not of her body, although you wouldn't know there is no biology there if you see their pictures. Holly went through a trial and a half taking this little girl from the nightmare of her existence to hope to family. I cannot tell the story nearly as well as Holly does so I will use her own words.

"The way I heard 'It's a girl' was different than most. Hard to believe it will soon be FOUR years since that first picture of our little Tazmanian Devil came through on my phone. She sure rocked our world - I've never had to work so hard at anything, but man I am so proud to be her momma. She has come so far - can't wait to see what this girl does. It's been one year since the worst day of my life. I was at work when I got a call that we had been expecting. We were waiting on a call to say that the parental rights of Taylor June's last parents had officially been terminated. (This is something these people WANTED and had set things in motion for this to happen a year earlier. We spoke with them two weeks prior for over an hour and everything was good to move forward with the adoption.) I excitedly answered the phone, greeted our case worker, and asked, 'How are you doing today?' Immediately I noticed her voice was not excited or celebratory. 'Well... I've been better Holly. Are you sitting down?' I laughed nervously and assured her I was. '[They] have changed their minds. They're flying down to get her tomorrow. We are just sick over it and are trying everything to stop it but I just needed to tell...'

"That's all I remember. The next thing I know 10 minutes had passed and I was outside of our building physically being held up by two coworkers, and with my office manager directly in front of me holding my face in her hands. I finally remember hearing her voice saying, 'Holly! BREATHE!! Holly! Look at me!' I remember opening my eyes to her being right in front of

me trying everything in her power to get me to stop crying and for my breathing to return to normal.

"Our adoption story is CRAZY. The things Taylor June went through and the way she made her way across the country to us is UNBELIEVABLE. When we were told about her, there were no 'what ifs.' If we agreed to adopt her, the process would start and it would be done. The probability of it not happening against our will was never a thought. So, unlike most foster- to-adopt stories, this type of outcome was never in the back of our heads. This little girl had been my daughter for six months. I had purposely assured her AT LEAST twice a day for four months in a row that she was home FOREVER. I repeatedly promised her I would NEVER let those people hurt her again. I made so many promises that I fully intended to keep and this would completely shatter all of it. I felt certain that after everything she had been through she would never recover from being taken from us and back to where she came from. This was her last chance in many ways.

"The fight of our life began. Except here's the kicker: Our hands were tied. There was nothing we could do (within legal limits) aside from letting our lawyers battle it out... except pray. We didn't want the kids to know about any of it so I had to put on a happy face with constant tears in my eyes and a lump in my throat. I would look at her and wonder if it would be the last day I got to see her. I would daydream about us attempting to go back to our old life before her, a family of four. I would have nightmares of what she would endure when she returned to the life she lived before us. I would jump up at every car that passed and check out of the window in fear that it would be them coming to ambush us.

"So, after I was able to put words into sentences, my coworkers called Lonny to come get me. He asked me what I wanted to do, and the only place I wanted to be was at church. Our pastoral staff met us there and I am forever grateful to them for comforting us and loving us in that time. I sat in the pews that Sunday before that phone call as our pastor preached on spiritual warfare. I could see the angels and demons fighting over this little girl's life in my mind. I knew it was out of my hands, which terrified me- BUT the advantage

to that was that for the first time in my life I put it ALL in HIS hands.

"The LORD will fight for you, you need only to be still." Exodus 14:14

"For the Lord your God is the one who goes with you to fight for you against your enemies to give you victory." Deuteronomy 20:4

"After eight days of anguish, we got the next phone call that I'll never forget... the call where she again asked me if I was sitting down- except this time her voice was different. This time she couldn't even wait for me to answer before she exclaimed, 'They gave up! God is so good!' The story didn't fully end there - we had many more hiccups and some 'super fun' events take place BUT - What Satan intends for harm, The Lord will use for good. He has tried to steal life from my girl numerous times and in many creative ways. I know she has a great destiny over her life, and I know the God of angel armies goes before her and fights her battles. One day she will have the faith to move mountains because she's seen them be moved before."

What a difference in Taylor June I see. She is overcoming her learning challenges and behavioral challenges that come from all the stuff that went before. She is becoming Moerer as we all should become More. 'Tis the season of giving and there is no greater gift than giving of yourself. I am so honored that I know and personally have had a chance to be a small part of the huge gift that I get to share with you today. These stories will make you smile and make you cry. From a room makeover for a sweet little girl to a brain training makeover for a precious young lady, these stories will highlight the moments that these families decided to change their family forever by adoption. This decision changed the lives of these families and their new members forever and they are all richer for taking the chance to BE the difference.

Maddelyn Russell

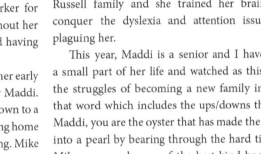

Maddi's story is one of long-term struggles with behavior and learning as well as with the home life she was given from birth with an incredible ongoing rainbow. My opportunity to meet Maddi was one I was not even aware would have impact upon her. A couple of her foster families brought Maddi in for testing as LearningRx many years ago and I noticed that she was dyslexic as so many undiagnosed children are. This was affecting her learning, which resulted in frustration boiling over into behavior problems. The social worker for Maddi's case kept noticing that over and over throughout her continuous placements, Maddi was getting tested and having the same report and the repeated behaviors.

Diagnosed with a recent health issue which caused her early retirement, Rhonda was feeling a tug on her heart for Maddi. She and her husband Mike were at the age of settling down to a quieter life, but she told Mike that Maddi needed a loving home and she just could not walk away without that happening. Mike said, "So what about us?" and there was the next part of our story. Rhonda and Mike brought Maddi to see me once again, but this time with the purpose of finding a change for this young teen. Maddi blossomed over the next nine months as she was formally adopted into the Russell family and she trained her brain to conquer the dyslexia and attention issue that had been plaguing her.

This year, Maddi is a senior and I have continued to be a small part of her life and watched as this family overcame the struggles of becoming a new family in all the senses of that word which includes the ups/downs that come with life. Maddi, you are the oyster that has made the world around you into a pearl by bearing through the hard times and Rhonda/Mike, you are heroes of the best kind because in your own words, "We didn't have a choice. The Lord put her with us in our hearts and we do the best we can." You did have a choice and you made it. Thank you for changing your life forever and changing my life through Maddi's journey.

we think. Tammy and John opened their hearts and home and stepped up to BE the difference. Annaiya came to live with them.

Annaiya Brownfield

In 2018 after some major life-changing decisions, my husband and I decided to attend a different church. This decision brought me into the interwoven story of Annaiya through a former client/friend attending this church with her family. Annaiya's birth mother has had a lifelong struggle with drugs and alcohol that had left had her in and out of jail and rehab for addictions throughout her children's lives from birth. In 2019, there were many changes and with the oldest child at 14 in state custody for ongoing juvenile delinquencies, she was arrested leaving her 5-year-old daughter with no one to care for her.

My friend Tammy and husband John saw the need in this young child's life and stepped up. They had been an extraordinary aunt and uncle to so many family and friends' children, even fostered two children years earlier. But in 18 years of marriage despite years upon years of prayers for a child of their own, they had finally accepted that this was God's plan for their lives and marriage. God's plan is different for us than

Their home was not ready for an active 5-year-old. This little girl had never even had her own bedroom, not even her own bed, before coming to their home. The legal struggles to get Annaiya a safe home with the Brownfields has taken over 18 months. Tammy said, "God's hands were open doors that were closed each step of the way." Just a few months ago, Tammy and John received permanent guardianship. Adoption is the next step in their process. Tammy and John have wanted to give this precious angel her "dream room" but that just simply was not possible with all the legal cost of guardianship and adoption.

Again, God opened doors and some people stepped up to BE the change and allowed me to be a part of this family's lives. Their story is just beginning to merge into a full family with all the intricacies of that dance. The powerful part of this story is they stepped up when the need was there. They decided to be the difference in a child's life and each one of the family members is growing in the journey. Just days ago, I was able to part of room transformation for Annaiya, along with gifts from LearningExpress Toys and some decorating help from my friend/colleague, Rhonda Waters, and Dalisa Hunt to give her that dream "unicorn" room.

Coleman Rounds

Being the difference sometimes means they are only with you for a few hours or a few days and it takes a really special someone to do this. Jacqueline Rounds is an amazing example of the fullest heart of caring that I know. The sweet senior has sacrificed her "retirement years" for a life of fullness and joy. Every time I see her face or hear her voice, she is a shining example of going beyond your own ability into that which God blesses you to do. I first met Jacqueline when she came to bring her son to LearningRx for an assessment/consult. She knew that this sweet young man needed more help than the school was able to provide and she was willing to be the difference at a huge sacrifice to herself.

That is when I first heard the story of Coleman. Coleman is a joy to be around. He is eager to learn despite his frustrations and Jacqueline shared with me that although she was in her 60s, she knew that someone had to be the difference in her community and in the lives of these little ones. She explained to me how she is a foster parent for kids both short term and long term, especially in the case of Coleman who she ended up adopting. "No child deserves to not have a family," she told me, "and as long as God gives me breath and I am able, I will be that to whomever he sends my way."

Often when I chat with her, she has an extra child or two in her arms or in sweet cries in the background. Sometimes they are only there experiencing her love for a few hours/days but she truly does spread that love and makes the ultimate sacrifice to be the difference. She recommends that if you want to be the difference, try donating gift cards for clothing to GeauxBags so those that do foster can get the children clothes when needed in middle of night.

Adoption or fostering may or may not be for you. I have known some amazing people with incredible stories to tell about them being the permanent difference for a child through adoption and some who have been a temporary foster care. The truth is that I cannot be either right now in my life so I take the opportunity to BE the difference in my life through my business by changing brains one at a time. My staff and I love to see the light of change come into children's eyes and even many adults when they finally read for the first time or learn something they have been working to overcome in math or in memory/focus. Brain training is life changing for so many and I am happy it is what I get to do each and every day.

The challenge here is the #Bethedifference in your world. If you can foster/adopt, step up and do so. If you can give to someone in need, do so. Ask about being a home for the holidays for a child who has aged out of foster care but has no home to come home to for the holidays. Give to a charitable foundation or resource such as www.topportunities.org designating the funds for a life in your community to be changed through brain training or other resources. Give the gift of learning to a child in your family or community who doesn't have the funds or needs some extra help. Whatever you choose. #Bethedifference this season for it is why we were created.

*LearningRx has gift cards that you can purchase in advance for those in need as well as partnering with VOA to access scholarship funds for those in need such as The Children's Brain Training Fund at the Community Foundation locally. Additionally, Transformational Opportunities at www.topportunities.org allows you to give anonymously to children/adults in your community to receive services such as LearningRx brain training and receive a tax credit for doing so. *Lola*

Finding *Joy*
When Nothing Makes Sense

What do you say to your children about what is happening to our country when you do not understand it yourself? How do you make sense of a world that has fallen off its rocker? In short, you don't. These things that are happening now to our world seem very chaotic and make us feel adrift, but the thing that we anchor to is where we go.

Children tend to anchor in their families when the world around them is chaotic and unpredictable so they will look to you for answers and the truth is the best thing for them to know, but not the whole truth nor the details of it. I remember the morning of 9/11 when I settled in my second-period class to teach reading ,and another teacher next door told me to turn on my TV, that history was happening. We watched in horror as the twin towers were struck, people leaped from windows to their deaths and the towers fell. My students all were silent and in tears as the unthinkable happened before them and yet there was a sense of unreality. The immediate impact and my actions as the teacher in those moments would stay with my students forever and how I addressed this at my own home with my own young children would impact them in their perceptions of security. I did what every person has to do in these unthinkable times. We have to set our minds on the things of truth. I told each one who was feeling completely overwhelmed that they were safe.

Safety is the highest priority in the fight/flight mindset that we get into when the unthinkable overwhelms our senses. We struggle for normalcy and a sense of peace because we believe those bring safety. These times we are living in make this harder and harder to meet but the truth is you are safe.

When you lose someone you love, the sense of security and peace is shaken to the very core and what you anchor to in those moments is where the peace comes from in these moments. In 2015, I watched my mother struggle with stage 4 breast cancer and I saw a woman who never wavered or had her sense of peace disturbed. She was like a placid lake that showed no ripple despite the hurricane force winds and pelting of boulders. I heard her say then that peace isn't the absence of storms in your life but rather the confidence in what/who you are anchored to during that storm.

What do your tell you children about the storms around you? You tell the truth and you tell them they are safe. One of my favorite songs says it best: "I've anchored in Jesus, the storms of life I'll brave. I've anchored in Jesus; I'll fear no wind or wave. I've anchored in Jesus for He has power to save. I've anchored in the Rock of Ages." If you look back at history, people have managed in much bigger storms than we have in our lives right now. The biggest part of our issues today come from the maelstrom of information and how it is presented. You are the anchor for your children until you give them their sea legs so that they might anchor independently of you. It is up to you to show them the how.

Steps to giving your children a sense of security when you feel overwhelmed:

- **Turn off the media!** The maelstrom of information load will completely overwhelm your life if you allow it and will bring with it a wind of negativity that you do not need. Not only is too much media bad for your brain but it is also terrible for your emotions and physical body.

- **Activity!** Play games with your family. Do a craft. Find some coloring books and color or grab large sheets and make a tent. Pretend play and create a sense of normalcy in the midst of the chaos around you. This will bring a sense of peace and joy even when the situation feels dire. One of the things I was always impressed with as a teacher is the child's buoyancy to the challenges of life. Bounce back with them. Let them bring some joy back to you. Go on a nature walk, a scavenger hunt. Have a scream fest where you go outside and scream as loud as you can.

- **Traditions!** Holidays look much different now and can be very hard as old traditions that brought a sense of security and joy are interrupted by loss and separation so start a new tradition. Put a puzzle together and then lay contact paper over it to make it into a placemat. Take something old and craft it into something new such as taking coffee filters and making them into angels to represent the ones you've lost.

- **Politics!** Embrace what is going on rather than avoiding it by taking the opportunity to use the teachable moments to discuss things like: what are politicians, who are our local ones, what is their purpose, how can we show our appreciation for them. I'll never forget doing this with my little ones after 9/11. We discussed who the firefighters and the police officers were and their jobs. My children wanted to make them brownies. We baked and took them treats monthly for the rest of their childhood and both of my children are now in that field as they valued their sacrifice so much.

- **Uncertainty!** Teach them to find what is certain in their lives and move outward from that. This will give them the ability to earn their sea legs for the storms of life. Freedom isn't free. This is an opportunity to show them the things that you value and how to appreciate those sacrifices for their freedom. Let them make cards, color pictures or make goody bags for soldiers who serve. Allow them to empathize with those who are segregated from community by making a small craft or item for those in nursing homes or for doctors/nurses who have given so much.

- **Prioritize!** Teach your child to recognize and prioritize people over things by giving something they value to another who is in need. Demonstrate the spirit of service by cooking a meal for someone in need and allowing them to help plan and prepare the meal or perhaps even shop for it if they are old enough. They can clean up the yard for someone else or volunteer time they have to others in need.

- **You!** Don't forget the You. Take time for you. Prioritize time to feel. If you feel overwhelmed and need someone to turn to, contact a counselor, pastor or licensed therapist to talk. Get a massage to ease the stress, even if that means rolling your foot or back against a tennis ball or rolled up sock because money is tight. Teach your child how to massage your neck/shoulders and show them that it is good to give relief and that you value their touch.

Making sense in a world that makes no sense or has very little of the sameness you recognize comes with adapting. This doesn't mean you have to give up your freedoms, but rather that you are willing to make some sacrifice to help another. Finding boundaries between self and others is a simple way to find joy. Jesus, Others, You. Put God first, others such as family, friends, neighbors and our country next, then yourself to spell JOY! *Lola*

BY DONESA WALKER, M.ED. BCCS, OWNER OF LEARNINGRX AND BRAIN TRAIN LEARNING SOLUTIONS

Soaring into Adolescence

Navigating the woes of Middle-School

The first time flying a kite is an experience of wonder and frustration until you begin to understand the power of the tether or line is what allows the kit to fly the best. Holding the line too tight will cause the kite to miss the wind and lose altitude. Being too loose with the kite makes it dance and dive but eventually crash.

Such is the balance of the line with teens.

My parents and I recently had a good laugh as I related how I was such a good teen and so easy to manage. I never got into "trouble," but I did have lots of ups/downs in moods. The laugh was on the part of my parents for what I perceived as such an easy time, to them was a roller coaster and the same is true with my boys who are thankfully on the "other side" of these years and into the next phase of life. The key to navigating the tween to teen years is in the tether.

BY DONESA WALKER, M.ED. BCCS,
OWNER OF LEARNINGRX AND BRAIN TRAIN LEARNING SOLUTIONS

The first stage of frustration reminds one a lot of the terrible twos…when the tween is just too little to be big enough to do what other teens do, but they are too old/big to do what little kids do, especially in areas of group events. This stage is fraught with body awareness and a desire to explore but not always in a safe or healthy manner and this requires the tightening of the string in order for that kite to catch the right wind and not get all tangled up with the other kites flying in all kinds of directions. The best advice for this is stage is to create boundaries and safety nets. Boundaries that are clear and enforced will allow the tween/teen to spend time with friends and provide a safety net of outs. This is a time that the child is really discovering who they are outside the parent. All of the new winds look so enticing and feel so exciting but without a strong tether will lead to a crash. For parents, the roller coaster of finding balance is so frightening and somewhat overwhelming that many become too tight and the child completely rebels and others let loose too much and the child flounders without boundaries. What are the right things to do? Build a kite and go fly it together.

1 Create the framework of kite together. Open the doors of conversation as a must daily. There must be times each day that the parent and the child talk -- really talk, not the text/call talk but the how I am feeling kind of talk. This is easier with girls most times as boys tend to struggle with finding the words to voice their feelings.

2 Cut the fabric on the pattern for the kite. This is a time to teach them the value of choosing the right fabric to build upon and the right tools to use to get where you need to get. This is the time you can discuss choosing the right friends and connections to begin planning for the future, setting goals and ways to meet them. This is time to begin opening the door to the ways you will be a different role in their future…a role that is much more demanding but very different.

4 Attach the tail string. Discuss the kite concept that you are there for their safety and for tether. Allow them to know that there are certain rights and privileges that they have but there are also expectations that must be fulfilled. Explain that you are their safety net and the tough call when they are in uncomfortable situations. I told my boys that I can be the bad guy you can blame all the no can dos on. Set up a security text word or even a letter that they can text you when they need you to get them out of a situation. Being the tether means that you can pull that kite in when the winds are too high, or they get too near the branches or power lines that would damage them.

3 Attach the tether string. Make an open channel of trust and sharing of expectations/non-negotiables. Allow the tween/teen to express their own thoughts and set the guidelines of dates/events/group gatherings/online chats/gaming/etc. together and allow them to input what discipline should be given for breaking the expectations you agree upon.

5 Decorate the kite together. Discuss how adorning themselves should be a reflection of who they are and not their peers or the current fads. Allow them to understand that while another person may want a kite/life filled with certain things, that these things are not who they are nor who they will be, so they need to fill their kite up with who they are and who they want to be in the future. My dad always told me the I was the mother of the woman I would become so I needed to remember that… and allow the person I wanted to be drive my life choices.

6 Put in the support bars for the kite structure. Be aware of learning issues and make sure you get these evaluated and treated as this is a time these often flare up when they have been hidden. Get support and testing from local experts such as LearningRx to know the baseline of their cognitive skills before they are involved in sports/driving/adventures that could lead to head trauma or learning issues. Recognize any issues with the emotional systems and reach out to local counselors. This is the time to teach them the value of support systems for using throughout life.

7 Go fly the kite together! Remind them that they are a part of you and always will be. Teach them the principles of the kite and the value of the tether. The principles and morals you have instilled from God's heart to theirs will still be there as long as they remember the value of the tether.

8 Be the wind beneath their wings. Provide opportunities for them to flourish and fly. Give them encouragement and plenty of opportunities to make good choices. Be like the mother bird who pushes the baby out to try its wings but is there to help the baby get back to the nest safely.

9 Repair the kite to fly again when it crashes or gets too close to a power line and burns. Reattach the tether when they cut it carelessly with their actions.

10 Fly with them for it will not be long until they are your tether, and you are the one dependent on them. Share that you too understand the value of the tether and that you will be the tether for them now as they will be your tether to this life by carrying on your legacy as life marches on.

Now, as Julie Andrews so beautifully sang…
"Let's go fly a kite, up to its highest height!
Let's go fly a kite and send it soaring…
up to the atmosphere, up where the air is
clear, oh, let's go…fly a kite! " (Lola)

Princess *Annaiya's* Fairytale Room

Annaiya Brownfield was recently adopted when a few of her "fairy godmothers" went to work on transforming the family's guest room in for a fairytale princess room. Annaiya wanted everything with pink and purple unicorns, so armed with wall stickers, new bedding and curtains to match, a new rug, ribbons, a special float, a unicorn pillow and some balloons from LearningExpress… Anniyas room was indeed fit for a fairytale princess.

One of the particulars she had asked for was a princess curtain, which was purchased and draped over the unicorn float to make a special reading corner. Curtains with fairy lights draped behind them gave the room an ethereal look. A special jewelry tray and unicorn lip-gloss complimented the dresser, where we added a little ribbon and some stuffed treasures to give the girly feel to the room. Tying strips of ribbon to the bed transformation gave it a magical feel and adding the special letter lights and wall decals made the room have zest and be a sweet surprise.

Annaiya was thrilled with the transformation exclaiming over and over in delight as she couldn't believe her fairytale dream had come to life. With a small budget and a couple hours of time the guest room became this little girl's dream room! Her surprise and delight tickled us as we were able to celebrate this child's transition from nightmare to fairytale life. Her life of struggles was changed by this family taking her to be their own and her dream room sprung to life with the touch of a few others who took a moment to stretch out their hands to inspire a little girl's future. After all, fairytales are simply dreams come true with a fairy godmother or two!

WRITTEN BY DONESA WALKER

Summer *Slide...*

IS EVERYTHING DESTINED TO GO DOWN THE **BRAIN DRAIN** THIS SUMMER?

I love sliding down slides with the curves and free fall experience of freedom, but I so do not want that ground to catch up to me as I have had far too many falls lately! I especially love the water slides in our Louisiana weather as they really combine the best of both worlds. What I do not love is the Summer Slide when it comes to education/academics and total loss of what has been learned. With Covid and all the negatives that were caused by shutdowns, the reality of slides in skills is all too evident. Summer slide or the summer slowdown or the summer brain drain as it is called is really a way to collective state the loss of overall content during a closure or time that the brain is not being stimulated at the same level as it is during a typical school year. The measure of the Covid shutdown was an astounding measure of over a year in reading skills and 8 months of math skills as estimated by an exponential case study based on summer slide measures in past and measured by student performance in classroom. The truth of the matter is that once standardized testing is completed, we will realize that the shutdowns cost our students much more in academic growth. Knowing there is a problem is only part of the issue, getting to the answer or a possible solution requires all of us.

BY DONESA WALKER, M.ED.,
BOARD CERTIFIED COGNITIVE SPECIALIST,
OWNER LEARNINGRX SHREVEPORT

1. While sliding in the park or playing in the water, engage in fun math activities such as counting backwards by twos or threes… avid swimmers who are older and more proficient can perhaps do dives to the bottom of the pool and come back up remembering the number…100 dive or slide, 97 dive or slide, 94 dive or slide …or even increase the spread to multiples of 6 or 7…100 dive, 93 dive, 86 dive…

2. Cookouts are a blast in the summer and even more fun is to cook with you kids. Allow them to use fractions to reduce or increase the recipes for a crowd. By allowing them to work with fractions from a young age to teen years, they not only gain those necessary cooking skills but the learn the fractions necessary for math and they learn that math is important to their future.

3. Read for at least 20 minutes a day and explore different places that house books from the library to the museum to the bookstore. Explore different types of reading from recipes to magazines to picture books and be sure to include audio books as this is good for listening skills and the underlying skills needed for reading as well. Choose to partner with local resources that have reading contests such as the community #chillandread contest offered by LearningRx along with community partners this summer… encourages reading in different genres

and locations while getting a treat.

4. Learn something such as a new hobby like fishing or snorkeling. Trying new things opens experiences for the brain and encourages challenges as well as an openness to learning for adventure. Try a new language like Japanese to celebrate the Olympics being in Japan this summer.

5. Review skills from the year in a fun and new manner such as some of the kinesthetic activities offered at www.blog.allaboutlearningpress.com. Instead of swatting flies or perhaps while swatting flies, you can also swat phonograms.

6. Sidewalk chalk play is a staple in summer. Go to the 101 Genius Sidewalk chalk ideas to crush Boredom at www.whatmomslove.com. Here you can learn ideas from letter hide and seek to water word painting that will take the summer learning to a whole new high.

7. Enjoy some geography as you travel or if you are doing a staycation, try out some geography fun from The Big Fat List of Summer Learning Ideas at *www.teachbesideme.com*. Geocaching is a great way to enjoy some outdoors and make learning a blast. It teaches map skills and lets you enjoy some fun with the littles.

8. If you absolutely need a guide to drive your summer learning, try out the Beat the Summer Slide Calendar of Activities

at *www.teacherspayteachers.com* which is full of printables and tons of fun.

9. Summer camps abound in great resources from the social interaction of stay over camps to the day camps offered by our local resources like SciPort and LSUS/LearningRx braincamps as well as individualized Crainium Camps for boosting those skills with a private brain trainer.

10. If you cannot take time away from the devices, which is the best advice I can give you to do…well, there are sites that are amazing too:

- *www.switcheroozoo.com*
- *www.funbrain.com*
- *www.kids.nationalgeographic.com*
- *www.reading.ecb.org*
- *www.starfall.com*
- *www.seusville.com*
- *www.storylineonline.net*
- *www.abcya.com*
- *www.highlightskids.com*

and many more…
www.learningworksforkids.com even has a list of video games that are good for kids!

The best advice is to take some time to be purposeful about learning and have a blast sliding into a great fall like into home base instead of losing what you've learned by doing nothing all summer.

the Reading Dilemma

Enough has been said in a negative fashion about the long-term results of Covid, closures and, and, and…the question is *what are we going to do about it as a community?*

For the team at LearningRx, we have decided to be a part of the solution by offering a great opportunity to encourage reading for all ages. We have partnered with several amazing local businesses to offer a summer reading contest - #chillandread! Each person who chills out with a good book can benefit with a chilly treat such as a fun cool slurpy or ice cream cone!

The fun reading chart is set up as a Bingo style, win-a-treat bookshelf where each time you complete 5 tasks in any order arrangement, you can come by LearningRx to claim your coupon for your treat! You can even combine the fun activities

into one awesome fun-filled day such as reading a book about history aloud to a friend while on a picnic to claim three of the five spots…add a bonus spot and score!!!

The required reading for school has never been so fun and this isn't limited to ages…you can read aloud to a toddler to allow them a chance to win and earn your own treat while doing so…the point is to encourage reading which is so good for the brain and in turn support our community through the amazing resources we have in our area.

While it is true that masks have caused students to struggle more with auditory processing which is the underlying skill needed for reading, it is also true that reading aloud to your family is good for your brain and theirs. Time to strike out and get a good book to chill with in our beautiful summer weather… **#chillandread** *Lola*

GO for the GOLD!

Setting Up Students Of All Ages For Success

DONESA WALKER, M.ED. LEARNINGRX OF SHREVEPORT

Dedication and practice are two recurring words that one will hear for every Olympian who is interviewed about their road to the gold. The best way to prepare for success is to be deliberate in setting aside the time to practice and to pursue it with dedication. No matter what the age of the student from toddler to adult.

FIRST, a designated area and time set aside for studying with healthy snacks and studying supplies is always a good idea. This can be as simple as a basket from the local dollar store with supplies in it so the student can pick it up when they come in the door to study and perhaps some type of signal that it is time to study/do homework or time to put up/clean up. Be sure this is an area with limited distractions unless you are deliberately training your student's attention skills in which case you can make it a game for them to ignore the TV and win a prize...

SECOND, a set amount of time. This is important because it allows the student to know that there is a beginning and an ending to this time. A reward for completing during this time can be appropriate if the child does not struggle but for one that does struggle with time management, an egg timer or stopwatch can help as well as perhaps a chart to show how long they spent on it. The right amount of time to dedicate to homework outside the 20 minutes of nightly reading that all students of all ages should do, is around 10 minutes per grade level. A first grader should have no more than 10-15 minutes of homework outside of the reading

2021 0809 Donesa Go for The Gold.indd   All Pages

and reading should be around 15-20 minutes. An adult can easily manage an hour of work plus an hour of reading if they do not have learning struggles but even adults can struggle with focus.

THIRD, providing adequate hydration and nutrition for studying is extremely important as studying is a laborious task. To encourage your child to eat healthy snacks versus junk, put a time price on them and make the junk cost more in terms of time. An orange is for ten minutes studying/doing homework without complaint but a cookie takes 20 minutes. Water is always free and readily available but juice or soda have a steep price tag!

FOURTH, CHUNKING! No, don't chunk the child or items at the teen…by chunking, I mean to break the work into manageable parts. Teens and Adults should be able to manage this for themselves but might need a reminder to do so. Young children will need you to help them break them work into manageable parts because after all the only way to eat an elephant is one bite at a time!

FIFTH, study tools such as graphic organizers, charts, highlighters, and grading sheets should be readily available and the student should be taught to use these. Starting early in the summer and creating a rubric for how you will keep up with grading and where you can post it/put it is a good idea. By creating a healthy atmosphere of learning from mistakes rather than seeing mistakes as failures, you can allow your student the opportunity to bloom into their own garden of learning styles. Take time now to practice study times, show the student how to use graphic organizers, charts and highlighters while studying. Read a chapter together in a book and create a test for the other person from the materials.

SIXTH, build Schema. This means simply that showing a student how to make connections is as simple as asking them questions as they begin the study process especially before a test. Ask these questions?

Have you ever seen or heard anything about this topic outside of school? Have you read about it before? How does it relate or have meaning to your life? Have you experienced this?

Making connections also allows you to encourage them into a positive growth mindset, which is a game changer when it comes to the overall learning experience. Having a positive learning experience at home can also negate the experiences that are not so great in other environments.

SEVENTH, note taking and organizational skills are not innately learned. These are skills that must be taught and trained. Use sticky notes, notecards, notebooks, etc. to teach your child organizational skills in note taking. Watch a video together then both of you take notes and show them that this is the way

to dump information down to a gist so that you can quickly go back and refresh before a test. Show them acronyms and mnemonics to help them remember these things such as the common ones like please excuse my dear aunt sally for math order of operations.

EIGHTH, problem solving. This is a skill that must be practiced from the simplest problem to the most complicated. Introducing everyday problems and showing the student how to solve them starts with scheduling conflicts, everyday tasks, cleaning a bedroom, etc. The student must be shown how to identify the problem, look at potential solutions and make a plan to solve, then solve.

NINTH, studying must have a method to the madness. This is a culmination of the previous skills. Choosing a methodical approach to studying is as simple as sitting down with this checklist and taking it one step at a time in implementation. Don't get overwhelmed, simply approach each step with a purpose and celebrate the achievements when accomplished.

TENTH, finally…Celebrate & Hire. Celebrate that you and your student are ready for a year filled with learning or Hire… come to LearningRx and hire a brain trainer to get your student ready for the school year filled with success and we will celebrate their accomplishments with you!

As Dr. Seuss so well said, "You are off to Great Places. Today is Your Day. Your Mountain is Waiting so Get on Your Way!" GO FOR THE GOLD!!! Lola

- ✖ **The noise is driving me crazy and I cannot function!**

- ✖ **I've struggled with this for years and still do but don't want this for my child.**

- ✖ **My boss just doesn't understand that I cannot process all of that at one time so I need a new job.**

- ✖ **I simply cannot pass the test to advance and need help.**

- ✖ **My attention has gotten so much worse and my memory stinks.**

WRITTEN BY
DONESA WALKER

[MIND SHAME]
YOU ARE NOT ALONE

Removing the Stigma for Adults with Learning DIsabilities

These are only a few of the things I hear from adults on a daily basis and surprisingly few of them are in my office. Actually, most are out in the public domain where people are feeling the shame of struggling but do not know how to address it. Let's shed some light on learning differences and move away from the clouds of mind shame.

What is mind shame?

Mind shame is a term, coined by the specialists at Children of the Code, where they have some amazing videos explaining the term for children/adults who struggle with dyslexia and understanding the code to reading. Essentially, the term simply means an extreme embarrassment at the inability to perform in the same manner as others around us. While that makes the term easy to understand, it is quite the deal to wrap your thoughts around the actual meaning behind this. Mind shame causes many expressions of emotion and turmoil not limited to anxiety and depression, attentional issues and guilt.

How do we address this culturally and societally?

Openness. Acceptance that not all people think the same and learn the same way and this is okay. The solution is getting help to make us feel whole. There is nothing wrong with a learning difference, but it can make it hard to function even if everyone around you is accepting of the difference. Why? Because most of us don't want to be different or to be perceived that way.

What help is available to adults struggling with learning issues?

Do you know what's causing it? Identify the why behind

the learning issue. This can be done through testing at a local psychologist if you want a formal diagnosis or if you are just wanting to identify the skills that are causing this struggle, you can come see us at LearningRx for a cognitive test. You can also call in or take one in the privacy of your home via computer. There is no reason for you to struggle silently wondering what is wrong.

Once you know what the root cause is and are comfortable with addressing it by getting brain training in-person or digitally, then you may also need to see a counselor for the grief, shame, guilt, anxiety or worries that the situation is causing or has caused you.

"Cindy" loved her job but felt very overwhelmed. She could not function with all of the distractions and auditory overload that was causing her to lose focus and be unable to feel success at her job. The situation was getting worse and worse. Finally, she decided after talking to a friend whose child had gone to LearningRx to call and see if they helped adults too. After testing, Cindy realized that her auditory input was being overloaded and she was completely losing focus due to the amount of auditory data that her brain was trying to process when it wasn't working at peak efficiency. After enrolling in a program with a personal brain trainer, Cindy began to understand her own brain and how to tune it efficiently when the auditory load became too much. She understands what exercises reduce her frustration and allow her brain to function at peak capacity. Yes, this is a blatant testimonial but the point is that instead of allowing the SHAME of not being able to cope to overwhelm her and cause her to leave the job that she loved, she was able to embrace that there was an issue and it could be addressed.

"Brad" struggled with managing his day-to-day schedule. He was constantly behind and although he owned his own business, his lack of management was impacting his home life and causing conflict in his family. He wanted to be able to achieve more balance and be able to do all the things he needed to do efficiently but his brain just didn't work like that. He went to a counselor who was helping him with the anxiety but the juggling of the jobs and home life was just overwhelming him. His counselor recommended that he get testing to identify what was causing the underlying issues. Brad got tested at a local psychologist's office and discovered that he had an executive functioning issue that was not allowing his brain to do the CEO duties efficiently. Brad chose to partner with his counselor to address this. He discovered that by taking some planning time in the mornings before he took off on his jobs, he could balance things better and complete jobs in a timelier manner. This allowed more home time with his family and alleviated the struggle. Again, this is an example of someone who took charge and decided for themselves that it was time to end the struggle.

"Cheryl" struggled with memory. She was known as the sticky note queen in the office because she had them everywhere to remind her of what was next. She had alarms on her phone and other reminders as well. But these things were beginning to get on the nerves of others around her and her boss complained that she was a disorganized mess. She tried to explain that it was just her way of managing but he insisted that she do "something about it." Cheryl decided to partner with a friend and work out a better manner for her organizational strategies. She consulted a professional who shared with her that she had ADD. Cheryl began to take medication for her ADD and with her friend's assistance, she was able to become the responsible person her boss deemed worthy enough to be promoted.

"Dallas" is a college student who struggles with math. She absolutely hates math and has had tutors for math her whole life. College math is a nightmare and makes her feel stupid. She is constantly putting herself down and has a mental block when it comes to anything related to math including her checkbook. Dallas is undiagnosed and makes it through the class with the help of the tutors but continues into adulthood avoiding math like the plague. When she has her first child, she is terrified of misdoing medication dosages and as the little boy grows up, she determines that somehow, he will get the help he needs with math so he doesn't struggle as she does. The crazy thing is, she is successful. She has multiple degrees and has been a successful teacher for many years. One day as she is doing research for her job, a parent introduces her to a new thought, brain training. And she embarks on the journey to finding this hope. If this story sounds familiar then, yes you guessed it. This is my story. I found LearningRx and it helped me discover math was not a disease after all. Learning math could be fun. Both of my boys did LearningRx and are successful in their lives and careers (that includes math). No, I am not an accountant...but I am no longer afraid of math nor do I feel insignificant and less than when it comes to math. Why? Because I took charge and did brain training for myself.

The point here isn't a LearningRx commercial but rather to share that taking charge of your own strengths and weaknesses is possible and knowing is all a part of that. Mind shame isn't something you should continue to deal with, but rather simply a limiting factor to what your potential can be.

No one should feel less than. No one should feel like they can't do whatever they put their mind towards doing. Embrace that there is hope. Reach out to others around you. Ask for help. There are community resources that can help you. Erase the shame and embrace your brain. *Lola*

Remembering the Purpose of the Holidays

Holidays can be highly stressful times full of angst and tasks. But, it is important that we focus on the reason behind the season instead of all the hustle and bustle. This year has added stress due to the supply of goods and toys held up in ports across our nation. What better time to refocus our energies on the why/what of the season rather than the commercialism of the holidays?

Here are a few ways to **repurpose your heart and brain** this holiday season including ways to stimulate your memory!

WRITTEN BY
DONESA WALKER

GET CREATIVE: Create games from common materials around your home. All homes have junk drawers! Pull one out and dump everything in a bag. Tell the kids or family members to use the stuff in the drawer to create a game for the family to play or create a new Christmas character who might have visited the manger.

TIME: Spend time with your kids and family. To a child, love is spelled TIME and you are their greatest gift! Take time to just be with them making memories. We all have each other. Making memories together is priceless!

FOCUS ON EXPERIENCES: Rather than spending on random things that likely will be forgotten five holidays from now, spend on experiences. This is especially important for the child/family member who has a love language of acts of service. Plan a picnic at Norton Gardens or go see the lights at The American Rose Gardens. You can make a coupon book of fun things to do throughout the next year together. Let your child anticipate these exciting things and plan when they get to do them with you.

VOLUNTEER: Take time this year to volunteer with your family at a local charity. Read aloud to kids in the classroom or serve at Maggie's Closet or Community Friendship House. Help other kids with homework after school at The Lighthouse. Spend time with Veterans who are in Veterans' Homes or at a day camp for Veterans through VOA. We are blessed in our area with many ways to serve others and this is a priceless gift to kids of all ages because it demonstrates who we truly are as a people.

EXPLORE NATURE: Have fun outdoors with the wonderful exploration of nature. Every yard has leaves, sticks and rocks, as well as other things. We have fabulous parks in our area, as well as beautiful lakes, rivers and bayous. Create a scavenger hunt for common things and let the kids have a blast exploring. For older adults and small children, you can do it hide and seek style inside the home by finding nature items and bringing them in, hiding them and allowing them to find them. Pick up pinecones, soak them overnight in water with Epsom Salt and red food coloring. Allow them to dry. They will become beautiful red pinecones you can decorate with or put on your firepit. You can also use them in your fireplace as a sparkler!

HAVE FUN WITH FOOD: Traditional food may be too expensive or out of stock for many so consider being creative with your holiday foods. Get a stick of butter and cut it into quarters. Allow kids to carve their butter into a holiday sculpture for decor. Or if butter is too precious, have them use a bar of soap and carve the nativity characters using a spoon. For unusual fun, you could dehydrate some food in the oven or over an open fire outdoors to demonstrate common practices for our ancestors in preserving food. You can create an unusual spread. One year, I did Grinch food. I simply colored a picture and stuck it to a popsicle stick and made common foods into fun foods. For example, I made a roast and called it Roast Beast and I called a mound of potatoes Grinch Hill. My family still recalls that Christmas as a huge hit! A few more that I did were: Who Hash (hashbrown casserole), Grinchy GreenBeans, Schlott's Knots (rolls), Diffendoofers (green deviled eggs with avocado instead of mayo) Crunchy Chicken Lickins, Beezlenut Splash (lime punch), Cindy Lu Who Salad, Grinch Fruit Kabobs (strawberry hat with banana slices and green grape for face arranged as a kabob on a toothpick)and Dirty Puddle Pudding (chocolate pudding). The point is just to have fun planning a themed menu or just use creative names for common foods to turn it festive.

STORY TIME: Take time to sit around the fire or living area talking and listening. Make some questions up in advance and have each person draw a question and talk about it or play would you rather. This boosts the auditory processing skills which are critical in listening and reading! It also connects the heart and mind causing big growth in the brain and social skills.

REDUCE ANXIETY: Practice "could be worse" scenarios when things feel out of control or by counting the blessings of what is in front of you. Get a simple jar and give everyone a piece of paper to write one thing they are thankful for, put it in a jar and read it aloud to all. This attitude of gratitude is especially great for mindset!

DRESS UP: Use what you already have and allow kids/others to play in your closet to come up with creative styles and have a fashion show. Be silly and enjoy the moments.

READ: It is fun to read the Christmas Story or the History of Christmas aloud. By doing this, your kids learn the patterns of reading and how readers read. Take turns reading by volunteers so that each person contributes. You can even print out or write out sayings, thoughts or scriptures to be read aloud. *Lola*

The point is that the holidays are truly not about the perfect gift nor the perfect decor, food, games, etc. It is about making memories that last a lifetime. Remember the true reason for the season. That an amazing God chose to send His Son as a tiny baby to the lowliest of all to show His incredible love for us.

May you have the merriest of all Christmases!

the *Right to* read

There are lots of discussions out there about voting and rights which are very important to discuss, but one simply cannot overlook the fact that over **80 percent** of Americans cannot read the ballot.

I know that is a stunning amount, but America is at an all-time low in literacy and due to COVID school closures this is a growing trend. Literacy at the fourth-grade level for America is below **50 percent** and only **12 percent** can read at a high enough level to get the legal language of a ballot. **Louisiana is 41st out of 50 states in literacy!** Unacceptable!

- Why then are we not challenging this right to pursue happiness and ease of learning?
- Why are we settling for the status quo?
- How do we make a difference in our community?

So glad you asked!

BY DONESA WALKER, M. ED.,
LEARNINGRX OF SHREVEPORT

According to The Literacy Company and U.S. Census Bureau, which underscore the critical need to address illiteracy in the United States:

- *Currently, 45 million Americans are functionally illiterate and cannot read above a fifth-grade level*
- *50 percent of adults cannot read a book written at an eighth-grade level*
- *57 percent of students failed the California Standards Test in English*
- *1/3 of fourth-graders barely reach the proficient reading level*
- *25 percent of students in school systems are able to perform basic reading skills*
- *85 percent of juvenile offenders have problems reading*
- *3 out of 5 people in American prisons can't read*
- *3 out of 4 people on welfare can't read*

The brain is a terrific tool but it needs stimulation in order to grow something as complicated as the skill of reading, especially in light of learning issues like dyslexia. Did you know that **2 out of 5** kids struggle with reading issues and **20 percent** of our population has dyslexia? Training the brain and identifying these weaknesses early is key to making change. Getting assessments on cognitive abilities and knowing where the child struggles can open the door to a world of learning. *How can you be the difference for your own child and those around you?*

The Literacy Project says, "If you're a parent and want a deeper dive at the situation, read below for a collection of stats in keys areas in child literacy to help prepare you to make a difference in the lives of your children:"

1. By **age 2**, a child's brain is as active as an adult's and by **age 3** the brain is more than twice as active as an adult's – and stays that way for the first 10 years of life.

2. Cognitive processes develop rapidly in the first few years of life. In fact, by age 3, roughly **85 percent** of the brain is developed. However, traditional education takes place in grades K-12, which begins at age five.

3. According to the Department of Education, the more students read or are read to for fun on their own time and at home, the **higher their reading scores**, generally.

4. **Reading and being read to** has an impact that extends beyond just hearing stories.

5. **65 percent** of America's fourth-graders do not read at a proficient level.

6. In a study of nearly **100,000 U.S. schoolchildren,** access to printed materials was the key variable affecting reading acquisition.

7. Children's academic successes at ages 9 and 10 can be attributed to the amount of talk they hear from birth through age 3. Young children who are exposed to certain **early language and literacy** experiences also prove to be **good readers** later on in life.

8. Books contain many words that children are unlikely to encounter frequently in spoken language. Books for kids actually contain **50 percent** more words that children are unlikely to encounter frequently than regular conversation, TV or radio.

9. The National Center for Education Statistics (NCES) found that children who were read to frequently are also more likely to: **count to 20 or higher** than those who were not (60 percent vs. 44 percent), **write their own names** (54 percent vs. 40 percent), **read or pretend to read** (77 percent vs. 57 percent)

10. Higher reading exposure was **95 percent** positively correlated with a growing region supporting semantic language processing in the brain.

11. The most important aspect of parent talk is its amount. Mothers who frequently speak to their infants have their children learn almost **300 more words** by age 2 than children whose mothers rarely spoke to them. Simultaneously, children learn the grammatical syntax and the social nuances around communication in their community.

12. Children exposed to fewer colors, less touch, little interaction with adults, fewer sights and sounds, and less language, actually have **smaller brains**.

13. The **number of books** in the home correlates significantly with higher reading scores for children.

14. Students who choose what they read and have an informal environment in which to read tend to be **more motivated, read more** and **show greater language and literacy development**.

15. Children who are read to at least **three times a week** by a family member are almost twice as likely to score in the top **25 percent** in reading compared to children who are read to less than 3 times a week.

ecoming the difference is possible! Talk to kids using big language not watered down. Volunteer to read to a local classroom or after-school groups such as Lighthouse with VOA or Community Renewal. Donate books to your local school for children to take home!

Thrifty Peanut Book Warehouse and *LearningRx* are partnering on a **Citywide Book Giveaway** on **March 2, 2022**, which is Read Across America Day! Everyone who lives in the area is invited to get a **FREE** book of your choice from Thrifty Peanut during that week of literacy. You can donate money towards this project by buying Thrifty Peanut Bucks and donating them to a local classroom or community group or even sponsoring a school! This is the start. These books can then be returned and exchanged for another after they have been read and enjoyed. Under this literacy project, our community can make a difference in the lives of our kids and others.

Reading is a right that everyone should have. The right to read whatever you choose. The right to hold a book that belongs to you. Literacy is critical to our future for without reading you are left to struggle in the abyss of the unknown world. Be the difference! *Lola*

The Science

"Learning to read" and "reading to learn" are phrases that we have heard for a very long time in education and publicly when discussing reading. However, as with everything, the basics behind the reading process are what is so important to know and understand. In the last couple of years, we have looked for details behind the science and I am happy to report that finally, those in the field of education are now learning more about the science of reading. So, what does that mean anyway? Let's discuss the cognitive skills behind the reading process and why reading is not a natural phenomenon but rather a learned skill that quantifies the ability of the reader. Since reading affects every aspect of our lives each day it is a necessary skill for survival. Now, let's dive into the science.

A letter is a symbol that represents a sound and when certain symbols (letters) are combined or arranged into a specific code, it represents other sounds. A spoken word evokes a picture in the brain which allows meaning to be attached to that word.

For super ease of expression, we are going to use the word CAT. When someone says the word cat, we can picture a cat in our brain but perhaps you do not realize that the cat you picture is the one you most recently or most often linked with that word. Your spouse, child, student or friend would likely describe the word cat quite differently than you do based on their own "schema" or memory experiences with the word/animal cat. The

more experiences and touchpoints to the word cat, the bigger your brain memory file is on that particular word and the more adaptability you have to accept new concepts or links to that word. And this is all just when someone says the word… this pictorial representation of the word cat happens in the visual processing part of the brain and those that are weak in this cognitive skill may struggle to connect the word to the pictorial representation. This can happen for students with visual processing issues such as visual dyslexia, as well as, those with traumatic brain injury due to illnesses such as COVID, PANDAS, brain trauma from accidents, strokes or dementia, as well as other circumstances. The speed at which one processes this information is also a critical cognitive skill that affects thinking and reading. If the uplink to processing is slowed by trauma, damage or weakness, this affects the overall function. When someone speaks a word to us, we must use a minimum of 4-5 cognitive skills to process that word for meaning and that is before we add the complexity of the

reading code in the English language.

Let's dive deeper. The letter C doesn't say C like an S when it is read but rather "c" like a k and the letter

A in the word cat doesn't say A like its symbol name either, instead it says a short vowel sound "a" and finally we have the T, that thankfully usually says "t" like the beginning of its name. WOW! That's a lot

WRITTEN BY DONESA WALKER

of Reading

for a three-letter word. Then one must blend the sounds together and link them in an orthographic picture to associate with the creature that has four legs, a tail, usually lives in a home with humans and meows. But I digress. I wanted you to understand that the process of reading has no simplicity to it at all but rather is a complex process of coding much like a computer must code the words that I type.

Let's simplify this discussion and get back to the science. With a plethora of research over the last 20 plus years, educators and cognitive scientists have discovered that there are many types of learning issues involved in the process of reading and the best way to teach reading is through a direct, systematic, structured approach that includes phonemic awareness, phonics, spelling and high-frequency words that follow exceptions to the code patterns. In 1986, Gough & Turner put reading into a simple formula view: D (decoding) x LC (linguistic comprehension)= RC (reading comprehension).

For simplicity, teaching explicitly to decode (including phonological awareness, letter-sound correspondence, and sight recognition) multiplied with LC (background knowledge, vocabulary, language structure, verbal reasoning, and literacy knowledge) weaves together into a strong ability to read. So this is why the cognitive skill function is critical to the process. If one struggles with memory then there is little to hold onto the codes and complexities. If one struggles with processing speed, then the person cannot think fast enough to process all of the different parts of the process efficiently. If the person struggles with auditory processing, then they may struggle to connect the code correctly to the sound. If they struggle with visual processing, then they are challenged with linking the orthographic representation to the sounds and/or the pictorial meaning. If one struggles with attention, then all of this can be challenged.

It is critical that we know how our brains and our cognitive skills are functioning. This is why cognitive testing is important at an early age and should be done regularly so that any changes can be monitored. It is easy as a parent to understand the concept of getting our eyes checked and our teeth checked so we should understand the concept of getting our thinking skills checked. Intervention is possible and is so effective with brain training at any age. The younger you start testing, the less of the struggle the student goes through and it is always easier to teach something right the first time than to retrain and unlearn compensatory skills. Brain training is truly life-changing for many. Reading is a process but it can be learned at any age. With proper intervention, it can open up a life of adventures and possibilities. *Lola*

DONESA WALKER, M.ED. BCCS, READING/DYSLEXIA SPECIALIST

RIPPLES

Written by
DONESA WALKER, M.ED. BCCS,
READING/DYSLEXIA SPECIALIST

f a dry surface has no drops of water, it is still dry. But single drops consistently delivered can become a river or even eventually, a flood.

The summer slide is a sad statistic that states that over 2.5 months of learning loss occur over summer. This is if no cognitive engagement is incurred and will mean that kids can start the year off behind. They can never really catch up it seems, but what about those drops of water? Summer sucks the hydration straight out of our bodies and brains, which leads to short term memory loss. But what about those drops of water?

Ripples in water come from one drop. One person who cares to make an effort. One drop of water can restore life to a plant, hope to a dying brain, or even begin the process of priming a pump. This can start the watering process. Recently, a person was commenting on all the negative things about our area. I asked one question: "So what are the solutions to all these issues you are concerned about?"

We can all ask ourselves questions. Where are *you* starting? What is *your* one drop? Here are a few suggestions to "hydrate" your life in order to get off to a fresh start to a new school year or just need a stepping off point.

 HYDRATE Drink plenty of water as it helps your brain, your body, your skin and your personality. Your demeanor is like a little cactus, try taking a sip of water every time you think of a negative thing to say. You'll either need to pee a lot or you'll learn to start thinking a little more objectively and positively. The ripple effect from a little hydration can get all your thoughts and memories flowing more freely allowing for a fresher perspective.

CELEBRATE You will find good if you look for it and it will ripple out to other people. Look for truthful things in other people to uplift them. Look for opportunities to smile, say a friendly word and lift others up because those ripples will continue to drift to others. This can cause a tidal wave of goodness back to you.

READ Choose a good uplifting book, devotional, webpage, or magazine that will stimulate your creative thinking. It can take you on a journey and inspire you to reach out to others. One word can ripple into a journey of a lifetime, giving you knowledge to share and grow on as well as refreshing those around you.

MEDITATE Pray and time to refresh yourself daily in good thoughts. This refocus/recentering yourself in priorities will often take the load of irritation off the brain and allow you to think with clarity and vision. A drip of time can ripple through you, giving you new insights and perspectives into yourself. As an added benefit, it helps your situations, even inspiring you to step out.

VACATION OR STAYCATION Find a local pool, river, or spring. Watch the wildlife, splash, swim and take time to just be. Skip a rock and watch its ripple effect. Play and enjoy life in its purest form. Take a friend or loved one along to create memories or go alone to relax. Remember to take a camera or your phone for a snapshot but be sure to put it away to enjoy the value of time.

VOLUNTEER Give time away to a VBS, camp, local library. Volunteer to read or babysit for a frazzled mom or mom-to-be. Sit with an elderly person or visit a nursing facility as well. The ripple effect of you giving time will pay back many times over. Your time may be the sweetest moment to someone who feels lost from their home or connections. Giving time is invaluable.

WATER Go water a plant, give life to something that is struggling to survive. Water a small business with your presence. Buy a gift for another. Go get a gift card just because. The watering you do to your community could be the difference in business survival within a dry economy.

SPLASH Go big. Get as lavish if you can. Throw a party. Doesn't have to cost a penny. Open your doors to your friends and family just because. Have Christmas in July. Celebrate life even if you only serve water. Gran a cucumber, freeze it, then add some mint leaves and add to water for a refreshing water party! Put the cucumber slices on your closed eyes for a facial reduction of puffiness. The ripples of life here can fade those wrinkles!

REST Take time to lay back in a tub of water and reflect on what you have. You have running water to refresh your skin, your soul, your being. Hydrate your body and dive into the water. Think deep and allow the ripples of rest to restore.

ENGAGE COGNITIVELY Do something good for your brain! Even though the rest of this list is ultra brain nutritious, be deliberate in doing brain exercises. For instance, saying your alphabet backwards while counting forwards by 3s or in the reverse. Recall as many items of food in your fridge that you can or list all the things that can be made with water.

Finally, take an ice cube and drop it down your back - That will certainly cause a ripple effect and maybe a laugh or a chuckle. But certainly a reaction!

Ripples come from the very first drop. There can never be a ripple if no drop is ever given. Join others, get a group, start a tide, a flood, a movement! However, start with a drop of goodness! *Lola*

Dyslexia, ADHD or Dyslazia:
Skill not will

The homework fight ensues again with the aggressive behavior and the meltdowns, the exhausting hours of fussing and sitting at the table, throwing tantrums and complete drama. When will it ever end? These are the comments and questions heard by many counselors and therapists as well as educational resource personnel on a daily basis. The question remains… is my child being lazy or are they truly struggling with learning issues? How do I know? The school says nothing is wrong, but I cannot do this anymore!

Dyslexia has as many as 9-12 types depending on which expert you are looking to and not all of these are addressed in the same manner at all. Dyslexia is usually defined as a processing issue of linguistic origin in a neurotypical person. However, there are neurodivergent thinkers who also struggle with the same cognitive weaknesses evident in dyslexic students of all ages.

WRITTEN BY
**DONESA WALKER,
M.ED. BCCS,**

The first step to understanding whether there is authentically an issue is by getting an assessment of the cognitive skills and looking at whether those skills are prevalently low or are there just gaps caused by interruptions in the learning process such as we see with the Summer Slide and Covid Learning Gap.

The second step is understanding the underlying weaknesses and choosing and interventional model that will best suit the learner and the family in getting the most out of the precious amount of time that you have with a child in the learning process.

Dr. J. Stuart Ablon in his book change*able, discusses how the lack of skill is the issue rather than a child willingly being defiant or lazy. In his book, Dr. Ablon, the Director of Think: Kids at Massachusetts General Hospital, shares how collaborative problem solving and realization/ intervention of skill sets can change lives at home, school and at work. Recognizing that weak cognitive skills (IQ) and weaknesses in emotional IQ or ability to handle new situations and adapt can affect a person's behavior whether the person is a child or an adult. The ability to recognize and address the weaknesses is one key to making change in daily lives. By identifying the underlying skill weaknesses in emotional

87

and cognitive thinking processes, one can become more aware and reach out by getting the assistance needed to address these underlying weaknesses. One video of his Tedx Talk, Dr. J. Stuart Ablon: Kids Lack Skills, Not Will to Do Well - YouTube, shares how training the skill boosts the motivation.

Another approach to this same principle is called Growth Mindset by Dr. Carole Dweck. In her book, MINDSET: the new psychology of success, Stanford Psychologist, Dr. Dweck coined the term "Growth Mindset" which says that adopting the belief that talent can be developed with hard work, determination and help from others promotes growth. Those with a fixed mindset, however, believe their intelligence and skills are innate and therefore unlikely to be improved upon. In her research, she was able to demonstrate that mindset matters and is trainable.   In

her multitude of talks, books, and videos, she shares her thoughts and research on how our perspective on learning truly matters. Teaching a Growth Mindset - Carol Dweck - YouTube. The human brain is always growing, changing, learning and the perspective that learning and growing should be a journey that is an adventure and fun is one that I hold along with many other educational professionals and cognitive scientists of all walks. Learning is an ongoing process of life and understanding one's own strengths and weaknesses in this process is a particularly important piece of that process.

Back to the question: is it a learning issue or a laziness issue?

Aren't they one and the same? Personally, I am lazy about doing the things that are hard and not enjoyable to me as most of us are. We do them only because they

must be done and some of us put it off forever (procrastinators), while others just do it to get it over with, (rushers). Learning should be about the joy of the process. School isn't fun to those who struggle because of their skills. Behaving, problem solving, dealing with difficult decisions, even cleaning the bedroom isn't always about unwillingness, many times it is lack of skill not will. Again, that first step is the knowledge of skill. Is the child, teen or adult who is having the difficulty unable to do or unwilling to do? How do you know? Have you assessed the abilities?

Dyslazia doesn't have to be the way of thinking. Overwhelmed brains do not have to be the norm. Meltdowns and shutdowns should not be commonplace. Addressing the underlying weaknesses and being purposeful in our approach to others can be life changing for everyone around us. If you or someone you love struggles with learning or behavior, no matter what their age, it is not too late nor too early. Intervention is possible. Reach out to community resources around you. Whether the person has a learning difference that needs to be addressed or they need to address behavioral concerns, resources are available in our community. 🅛🅞🅛🅐

A Holiday Gift
for the Brain

THE GIFT OF READING STARTS IN THE BRAIN, NOT IN THE CLASSROOM!

xcitement spread across the face of my daughter-in-law as she opened the present and saw the books! She smelled them and hugged them for they meant that she was getting to go on an incredible journey soon and I knew exactly what she was feeling because that is the way I feel in the presence of books. My husband looked at both of us like we were crazy! He said, y'all remind me of this girl who I went to school with who was so excited the day the teacher announced we were going to learn cursive writing and multiplication. He said, I was thinking here I am stuck in the minimal correction facility every day

instead of getting to be outside hunting and fishing and she's excited? The difference is the joy of learning!

Learning to learn and enjoying learning is an incredible gift which I know from personal experience because it is a gift that I get to see unwrapped every day! The process of learning starts in the womb as the brain forms synaptic connections and patterns that begin to fire together and wire together making connections that will last a lifetime. A child can tell its mother's voice at birth because it is a familiar pattern and cadence. "Talking, reading, and playing a variety of music can help stimulate baby's senses and improve brain development while in the womb", according to Dr.

Michael Roizen. "Exposure to different sounds and scenes is essentially what helps establish connections from one set of neurons—the nerve cells of the brain—to another. This is how we all learn." One study even found that saying a fake word over and over in late pregnancy boosted the child's ability to discern that same word after birth. They could discern this by neural signals emitted by the babies that showed they recognized the pitch and vowel changes in the fake word. The babies who heard the recording most frequently displayed the strongest response, suggesting that infant language learning begins in utero. So exactly when should you start reading to your baby in the womb? At about six months along, a baby is already quite familiar with the sounds of the womb, from the mother's heartbeat to digestive sounds. From outside the womb, sounds are extremely clear, although about 10 decibels lower. This is just the beginning of the gift of reading and loving to learn.

When should you stop reading to your child? NEVER! Many parents assume that once the child begins to learn to read that they should stop reading to them and this is a myth! Reading aloud is one of the most powerful ways to pattern reading and the way that readers solve issues in reading. I encourage all parents to read chapter books above the children's reading levels as this introduces new vocabulary as well as word attack skills, enunciation, characterization, interactions with the texts and so much more.

The journey to reading must be approached in a scientific way to make sure the brain has the necessary skills to implement the reading process. After all, reading doesn't start in the classroom, it starts in the brain. Many cognitive skills are required for the process of reading including but not limited to auditory processing skills, memory, and processing speed. Addressing all of the core cognitive skills starts with knowing which skills are weak and which skills are strong. Let's examine just one word in this process: cat. The brain must recognize the letters visually, connect them to sounds, they make when combined in that particular code, blend those sounds then access the stored file of memory linked to that word to connect the sound/code/word to derive meaning. All of this happens in nanoseconds when the brain has automatized the process of reading but takes time when the learner is still new to the process. Each letter is associated with multiple sounds when combined in different combinations. Even though we only have 26 letters, the English language has over 44 sound combinations in our linguistic system not including the words we have incorporated from other languages. This makes the challenge of reading the greatest feat a child accomplishes in their young years. Did you know reading requires more brain power than walking and requires a lot more training? Most people are unaware of this and assume that this is something the school just teaches and the kids pick it up naturally but the process of language encoding and decoding is not a natural process like speech. Even with speech we spend time training our kids to enunciate and correct their sounds or we would all walk around calling water by a different name like wawa!

If a child struggles with vision, we take them to an optometrist and get them glasses or other assistance. The same can be said for hearing and audiologists, illnesses and pediatricians or specialists and dentists and teeth. So why then are we so prone to ignore the brain and understanding the strengths and weaknesses, going to a cognitive specialist for a quick checkup and diagnostic then getting assistance to help ourselves be as efficient at learning and reading as one can be? Is it time you had a brain checkup for your child's learning abilities? Why should a child struggle to learn to read when identifying the weak skills in the brain and addressing them early on could set them up for success in he classroom? Give the gift of reading and learning for a lifetime! *Lola*

WRITTEN BY
DONESA WALKER, M.ED. BCCS,
LEARNINGRX SHREVEPORT

BABY STEPS
to a Healthy Brain in 2023

Healthy:

<u>H</u>ydrate Constantly

<u>E</u>at Well

<u>A</u>ttitude of Positivity

<u>L</u>et it Go to Sleep

<u>T</u>hink, Meditate, Pray

<u>H</u>elp Others

<u>Y</u>our Exercise

Hydrate Yourself Constantly to Reach Optimal Brain Health.

Your body uses an enormous amount of the water you take in, but your brain uses more. If you are not providing the right level of hydration for your body, then your brain is starved for the fluids it needs, like the gas in an engine. If you are not supplying enough fuel for your body and brain to function correctly, then you may experience memory loss, especially in the short-term memory area of the brain. There can never be enough said about the importance of H2O.

Eat Healthy Foods, Especially Greens Rich in Magnesium, for a Smarter You.

The brain needs magnesium to build and grow. Eighty-five percent of Americans are magnesium deficient simply because they do not eat enough foods that provide this critical mineral for the brain. Magnesium is one of the essential minerals for the brain, but it is not the only one necessary for brain health. While it is very important to eat foods rich in nutrients to promote physical health, meal times can also boost your mental health. Taking time to have a meal rather than through can be game-changing. Sitting down for a meal with the whole family is a great way to build communication and socialization in young children and adults alike, especially seniors, where socialization is critical for the brain.

Attitude of Positivity

A positive attitude is transformative for the brain. Research has shown that IQ scores can be changed by as much as ten points with positive reinforcement and belief in oneself. One way to improve self-esteem is to look in the mirror and state five positive facts about yourself. This exercise can increase your belief in your ability and your confidence. I call this the Wonder Woman or Superman effect. Knowing that you can is a large part of the battle of self. This process starts with believing that you can, even if you are not quite there yet. Recognizing the growth mindset, or the ability to change and grow, has been proven to be the biggest factor in making significant changes in the brain. If you cannot do it yet, that three-letter word becomes very important—Yet. It does not mean that it is impossible forever. At that moment, it is potential energy, a possibility for the future, something that can be achieved if you put your mind to it and want it badly enough.

Let it Go and Sleep Deep for a Healthy You.

The most significant factors that impact the brain are stress and lack of sleep. Both of these elements are critical for brain health. Reducing stress is essential for good sleep, and deep sleep is good sleep. Deep Sleep is the key to reducing stress. A media diet is a significant component of good sleep and stress reduction. A media diet consists of no more than ten minutes of streaming media multiplied times the age of a child and no more than three hours for an adult. A complete hiatus, or no media consumption, is recommended beginning one hour before bed, especially streaming media. This media break helps your brain reach REM sleep and rest deeply. Sleep is a restorative process for the brain allowing stress to be released and many problems to be solved that the brain has been working on all day. As Queen Elsa says, "let it go." Neither frozen pipes nor pipe dreams bring about great health. Instead, climb into bed and let it go.

Think, Meditate, & Pray for a Creative Brain.

Many people think meditating or praying is all about getting rid of stress. The truth is these are thinking processes that are critical for creativity. Meditating, praying, and deep thinking allow the brain to reach beyond and think of other possibilities outside itself. These techniques allow the creative juices to flow in art, music, science, religion, and other areas of our society. Focusing on things beyond our control and what our mind can grasp in this finite world allows our brain to imagine the possibilities of a brighter future. A sense of wonderment and belonging happens from allowing the brain to meditate. Pray and think deeply without being task driven. This time of peace allows the brain to put new materials in and make new connections previously not seen or fathomed. This is the reason why play is so critical for children, from recess to imaginary play. We forget as adults how important it is to play. We need to have adventures, laugh, enjoy and create. These joyful and creative activities get our brains firing and wiring and relaxing and growing.

Helping Others

Being helpful leads to a more connected brain with better longevity and less memory loss. One of the most critical factors in avoiding dementia is to stay connected and socially active. Helping others in our society, neighborhood, and other realms of influence allows us to construct and learn new things more effectively and efficiently. The more we reach out to help others, the more we engage our minds as we learn new things, meet new people, and change. Our society benefits and grows from one person helping another. This is exactly how our brains make connections and neural networks. Getting outside yourself and outside your comfort zone to try new things with new people creates new memory banks, new connections, and new neural pathways. A constantly adapting brain assists with the memory processes. When neurons repeatedly fire together, they wire together, which helps prevent dementia.

Exercising Your Brain and Body Makes a Healthier and Happier You.

Exercising is necessary for both the brain and the body. Getting outdoors and connecting with people and nature by participating in activities like gardening and taking walks is exceptionally valuable for your mental and physical well-being. All these things can lead to a healthier brain and a healthier you.

It is easy to read an article like this and say, "Wow, I already do those things, or I've done those things in the past, but I haven't really noticed any difference." If you are doing these things, then I encourage you to continue. You may not have noticed a difference because you are a healthier you in both brain and body. If you are not doing these things, start wherever you need to start. For some, that might be simply drinking another cup of water each day, doing a fun activity, or going out to lunch with a friend. Some may need to look at themselves in the mirror and realize the wonderful human being God created is there looking at them. Some may need to eat a little less or perhaps a little healthier. Some may need to stress less, sleep more, and pray a lot more. Wherever you find yourself, I encourage you to find the healthier you and embrace that person in 2023. (Lola)

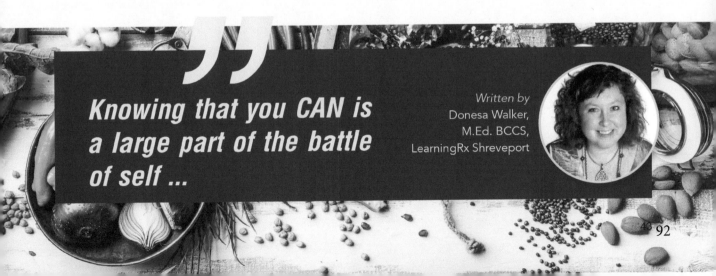

Knowing that you CAN is a large part of the battle of self ...

Written by
Donesa Walker,
M.Ed. BCCS,
LearningRx Shreveport

E-X-T-R-A-ordinary!

The question is asked: why be the ordinary when you can be the extraordinary? What is the difference between ordinary and extraordinary?

It's the extra of course. In a world with so much technology, advances, and things that are catching people's attention, how do we become extraordinary and stand out? What is it that makes the difference in the lives of those people around you? It's the extra. Lately, many of my sweet friends and people who mean a lot to me have left this ordinary life for a different journey and so I have become pensive by looking at what makes the difference. My favorite bird is the peacock. But the peacock is just a bird. It doesn't even really fly. The peafowl can fly but not him. He walks around and does all the other things that other birds do and yet the peacock is seen differently, why? It's the extra of course the peacock is overly dramatic and its behaviors, and in the tail that is just extraordinarily beautiful, large, and in charge. I've always loved the peacock for the colors and the vivaciousness of it but I have loved it more because of the extra. What is the extra? In the peacock, the extra is that 60% of the bird is in the feathery tail that he uses to draw a mate. That is the beauty part that fascinates us.

The extra is the perception of the peacock as Outgoing, confident, and friendly. Peacock personalities are warm and entertaining, which can become dramatic under pressure. These people are motivated by recognition, applause, and acknowledgement/acceptance. Peacocks live by the mantra: "Hey, world – look at me!" Imaginative and noisy, Peacock personality people thrive when they can openly share their ideas and feelings. I might be a peacock, but the extra is what I strive to be. What is the extra that makes the extraordinary? Most people don't realize that it is the extra that makes your brain rewire such as trying new things to become creative and grow. When we challenge ourselves to stretch out of our comfort zone and become more than what we are used to being; when we feel tapped out and yet we go the extra mile, that's when we get true growth. Muscles only grow when you push them beyond what their actual capacity is; not a lot because that will cause damage, but just a little, just a little stretch, just a little more of what you have given to those around you. So, let's examine the extra.

Written by Donesa Walker, M.Ed. BCCS, LearningRx Shreveport

E stands for Excellence. This conveys excellence and customer service, friendship, provision, or just being there in a quiet and steady manner excellence means doing more than is required. In today's society, excellence stands out, because so many are settling for the ordinary. Excellence means that you go the extra step, go the extra mile, be willing to take that phone call, that extra minute to listen, that time, that effort to be the difference. Many have asked what makes my business so extraordinary and it is because of my staff and their willingness to go to excellence no matter what that takes. *Research link: Excellence through Mind-Brain Development: The Secrets of World-Class Performers*

X stands for Xenacious which means eager to try new things and being willing to stretch ourselves outside of our Normal. Being xenacious means trying to be more than who you are and this is a powerful way to grow your brain. When the brain is learning, it builds new synapses and grows. This is how the brain stays healthy and active by learning new things whether that be a new language, a new way to do things, a new location, or any type of stretching outside of what the brain is used to doing. Research link: The hidden pattern that drives brain growth | Stanford News

T stands for Tenaciousness. There are over 385 words in the English language that stand for being terrific, amazing and good but none of them hold the candle to tenaciousness. Being tenacious, or having tenacity means to hold on to what is good, even when things are going bad. Another word for this as far as brain growth is called grit. Dr. Carol Dwyer has done a lot of research when it comes to grit and the incredible value that it has in determining future potential and the ability for the brain to grow and change. In fact, she has coined the term growth mindset. The growth mindset is one that has tenacity or grits, and is willing to work through difficult times, holding onto hope or believing that better things are coming. This growth mindset is always looking for the next thing to change grow, and become so that the brain can get more, and be more, the growth mindset actually is one of the major determining skills and the ability to be successful in life even more than IQ alone. Tenacity or tenaciousness has been lost a lot in today's society where we jump from one thing to the other when it's uncomfortable or we don't like the experience. It is very important to the brain that we learn to work through difficult circumstances and stick with it despite it not being a fun thing or even something we fo not see great value in doing. This is especially important to young children when being enrolled in sports or other activities. Parents should not allow them just to quit because it is difficult or hard, but instead teach train them in tenacity and growth mindset by making them go through the process of sticking with it. Many adults still need to learn this themselves. The extra tenacity pays off in the long term. Research link: Developing Resilience, Tenacity, and Grit

R stands for Real. While our could easily stand for radiance, refreshing renewing and resilience stands for real because the truth is often lost in our day today lives and real means that we stand the test of time. One of my favorite books growing up was The Velveteen Rabbit. The velveteen rabbit was just a little stuffed animal given to a small child as a toy. In the story, the rabbit only became real by enduring all the difficulties of life, and it was actually through hard circumstances, and being discarded that the velveteen rabbit came to life as a real bunny. The truth is that the extra in being real means being open, truthful, and frank. It means not hiding behind other things but being willing to take the brunt of someone's frustration, being willing to say yes, I did that to hard things or no, someone else deserves that honor when they are the one who did the work. In the world of Fakebook, most people really appreciate things that are real, and they can rely on. Experience matters. Developing the brain requires real life experiences and one interesting thing is that one cannot lie to oneself so real becomes extremely important in the extra of ordinary life. Research link: The Role of Experience in Brain Development | Better Brains for Babies

A stands for Affirmation. Affirmation is incredibly positive and incredibly necessary for the brain. This is how the brain knows that something is to be done again and again, because it receives rewards affirmation, and this builds confidence. Technology has been built with this in mind. In fact, one of the most addictive things about technology and iPhone in particular is because they are constantly rewarding the brain which makes this highly addictive to the brain. Affirmation is a trait that can change behavior and change the way we do things just by the right things being affirmed in our lives consistently. This can be by surrounding yourselves by positive people, positive words, uplifting things, and consistency. The extra and affirmation is being willing to affirm the good things in the lives of the people around you, and in your own life. Look in the mirror, affirm who you are, and who you want to be daily and watch it happen. Research link: *https://www.researchgate.net/profile/Golnaz-Tabibnia/publication/323707692_Resilience_training_that_can_change_the_brain/links/5f2430e692851cd302cbabed/Resilience-training-that-can-change-the-brain.pdf*

Being ordinary isn't a bad thing. But being extraordinary is a terrific thing. The extra is just stretching yourself, and those around you to become more, do more, be more, strive for more, want more in life not things and desire more of the good from all around you. So back to my question: why the ordinary when you can be extraordinary? *Lola*

Milton Keynes UK
Ingram Content Group UK Ltd.
UKHW051015270923
429452UK00003B/52